A DAY

IN

ANCIENT ROME

BEING A REVISION OF LOHR'S "AUS DEM ALTEN ROM"
WITH NUMEROUS ILLUSTRATIONS

BY

EDGAR S. SHUMWAY

PROFESSOR OF THE LATIN LANGUAGE AND LITERATURE, RUTGERS COLLEGE
PRINCIPAL OF CHAUTAUQUA ACADEMIA OF LATIN AND GREEK

*" From the very soil of silent Rome
You shall grow wise; and walking, live again
The lives of buried peoples." — J. A. S.*

*" Rome est cause que vous n'êtes plus barbares, elle
vous a appris la civilité et la religion." — BALZAC.*

FORTY-FIRST THOUSAND

BOSTON, U.S.A.
D. C. HEATH & CO., PUBLISHERS
1893

Other Publications of EDGAR S. SHUMWAY:

A Hand-book of Latin Synonyms.

The *Latine* Parsing and Analysis Tables (*in Latin*).

Lists of Words Occurring More than One Hundred Times in Cæsar and in Cicero's Orations.

Comparative Tables Showing the Minimum Requirements in Latin and Greek, by some twenty
Representative Colleges and Universities, for the Degree A.B. (1887).

Latine et Grace: Volumes I.-IV.

CONTENTS.

	PAGE
Roma Antiquissima	4
Corso	5
Plan of Modern Rome	6
The Campus Martius	7
Head of Marcus Agrippa	8
The Pantheon	9
Equestrian Statue of Marcus Aurelius	12
The Capitoline Hill	13
The Story of Tarpeia (Livy)	14
Temple of Jupiter Optimus Maximus	15
The Destruction of the Temple (Sulla)	17
The Roman Citadel	18
The Forum and a Triumph	19
The Forum in Festal Attire	20
The Carcer	21
The Tullianum	23
The Imprisonment of Jugurtha	24
Arcus Septimi Severi	25
Caracalla	26
Templum Concordiae	27
Cicero's Third Oration against Catiline	28
West-end Forum, time of Domitian	29
The Umbilicus	30
The Golden Milestone, The Græcostasis	31
The Temple of Saturn	32
The Temple of Vespasian	33
The Column of Phocas (Marc Antony)	35
The Imperial Rostra (Trajan)	37
The Marble Barriers	38
The Public Schools of the Early Period	39
Story of Virginia (wax tablets)	40
The Forum	43
The Basilica Julia, Temple of Castor	44
Battle of Lake Regillus	46

	PAGE
South-east Forum	47
Divus Julius (Caesar)	48
Atrium Vestae	49
Horace's Adventure	51
Arch of Titus	54
Caligula	56
Portion of Palatine	57
House of Cicero (Hortensius)	59
The Germalus	60
The Domus Gelotiana	62
Hadrian's Paedagogium	63
Roman Lads at School	64
The Coliseum	68
Vespasian	69
The Circus	70
Septimius Severus	71
The Stadium	72
Augustus	74
Domus Tiberiana (Tiberius)	76
Interior of a Roman House	77
Galba (Residence and Death)	78
Otho and Vitellius	79
How Domitian Built his Palace	80
A Reception at Domitian's	81
A Roman Garden Scene	82
The Emperor's Court	83
Nero	84
A Visit to Domitian's Triclinium	85
Statius and his Poem	86
The Garden	87
Domitian	89
Temples of Jupiter Victor and Jupiter Stator	91
Death of Caligula (Claudius)	93
Rome from the Janiculum	95

Press of Berwick & Smith, Boston, U.S.A.

PREFACE.

IF some liberty has been taken with Dr. Lohr's "*Aus dem alten Rom*," it has been either in view of more recent excavations at Rome, or for the sake of illustration or greater perspicuity. Perhaps it will be pardoned me if I seize the opportunity to press upon any reader who is not yet a student of Latin the practicability as well as desirability of an acquaintance with Latin literature—

> " Tully's voice, and Virgil's lay,
> And Livy's pictured page "—

and that too not through translations and special treatises alone, even if so attractive as Dr. Wilkinson's admirable "After School Series," but in the Latin language itself. Weighty are the words of Schopenhauer : " A man who does not understand Latin is like one who walks through a beautiful region in a fog; his horizon is very close to him. He sees only the nearest things clearly, and a few steps away from him the outlines of everything become indistinct or wholly lost. But the horizon of the Latin scholar extends far and wide through the centuries of modern history, the middle ages, and antiquity."

May this little book prove not only an aid, but even an incentive!

Acknowledgment of assistance is here made to Mrs. Minna V. Fitch, to Miss Katharine H. Austin for her translation of Horace's ninth satire, to Mr. Samuel M. Otto of the Chautauqua *Academia* of Latin and Greek, and to Mr. Sherman G. Pitt and Mr. Melvin D. Brandow, students at Rutgers College.

EDGAR S. SHUMWAY.

RUTGERS COLLEGE,
NEW BRUNSWICK, N. J.,
  June 17, 1885.

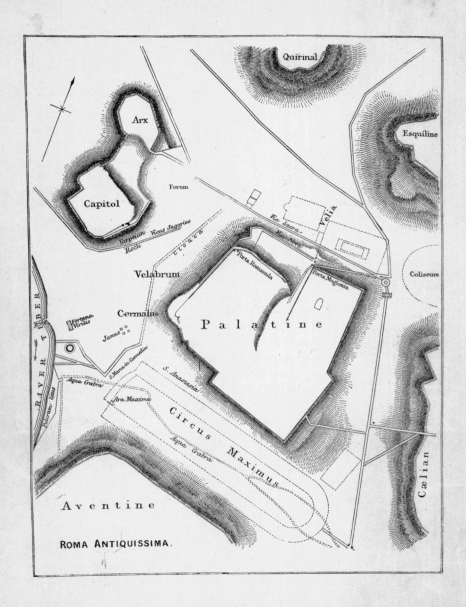

Quirinal

Esquiline

Arx

Capitol

Forum

Velia

Coliseum

Tarpeian Rock

Vicus Jugarius

Cloaca

Via Sacra

Via Nova

Porta Romanula

Porta Mugionia

Velabrum

RIVER TIBER

Fortuna Virilis

Cermalus

Janus

Palatine

S. Maria in Cosmedin

Pulcrum litus

Aqua Crabra

Ara Maxima

S. Anastasia

Circus Maximus

Aqua Crabra

Cælian

Aventine

ROMA ANTIQUISSIMA.

A DAY IN ANCIENT ROME.

N Rome I often think of you, and wish you, too, might tread the squares and streets through which have walked the Roman authors whose works you are studying, as well as the men of whom they speak.

The Latin historians, orators and poets, from Nepos to Horace and Tacitus, would become much more familiar and dear to you if you could see where they lived and wrote. And, out of the dead letters, living forms would arise, if you could read them in that place to which they carry you in spirit, that is, in Rome itself.

Perhaps I can, in a measure, make up for your loss in not being able to see these places, by telling you what letters and stones here have told me. But, to follow me aright, you must direct your thoughts (you know they are always ready for a flying trip from the class-room) toward sunny Italy. Fancy you are visiting me here, every one of you; whither, then, should I rather lead you than to the central points of the old city?

To take our bearings as speedily as possible, let us go to the *Corso*. This is the most animated street of Rome, and runs in a straight line from the *Porta del Pŏ'polo* to the *Piazza di Vene'zia*. It

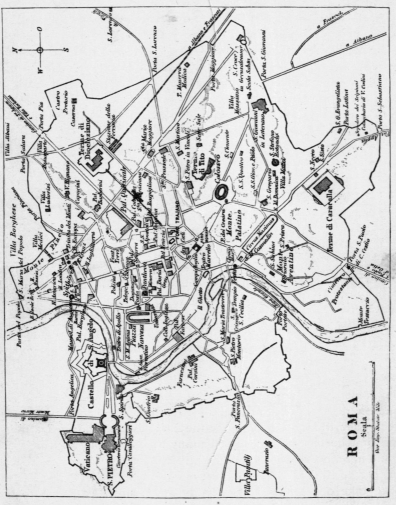

PLAN OF MODERN ROME.

corresponds toward the north with the ancient *Via Flamin'ia*, and toward the south with the *Via Lata*.

It was once spanned by the triumphal arches of Marcus Aurelius, Domitian and Claudius, but they have all disappeared.

By this street we cross the *Campus Martius* (Field of Mars), the great play-ground of the ancient Romans. Here the young people ran, wrestled and fenced, or played their favorite games of ball. As it is the custom among the better classes in Rome to-day to take a promenade or pleasure-drive in the *Corso* in the afternoon, so the ancient Romans, after business hours (*"post decisa negotia"*), resorted to the *Campus Martius*. Horace is one of the more sensible ones: he goes to the bath when the heat of the sun becomes too oppressive:

> *" Ast ubi me fessum sol acrior ire lavatum*
> *Admonuit, fugio campum lusumque trigonem."*

> " And when the sunbeams, grown too hot to bear,
> Warn me to quit the field, and hand-ball play,
> The bath takes all my weariness away."

Though, to be sure, Shakespeare speaks of a more vigorous swim in the Tiber, at this spot:

> " Once, upon a raw and gusty day,
> The troubled Tiber chafing with her shores,
> Cæsar said to me, ' Dar'st thou, Cassius, now
> Leap in with me into this angry flood,
> And swim to yonder point ? ' Upon the word,
> Accoutred as I was, I plungèd in,
> And bade him follow—so, indeed, he did :
> The torrent roared ; and we did buffet it
> With lusty sinews ; throwing it aside,
> And stemming it with hearts of controversy."
>
> —*Julius Cæsar.*

But serious matters were also undertaken in this extensive "field." Here the people assembled (for *contiones* and *comitia*); here they voted for candidates for the office of Consul. Of the two chosen, the one was usually a man of approved character, and belonged to the better class of the nobility; while the other had in attendance a larger number of adherents (so-called clients).

MARCUS AGRIPPA.

During the time of the Republic a rude enclosure, much like a sheep-pen, sufficed to keep in order those who came to vote. Cæsar began to substitute walls of marble, and Marcus Agrippa completed them ("*Saepta Julia*"). After Cæsar's time, Agrippa gave this place an entirely different appearance by his magnificent baths. The public buildings, however, were soon surrounded by private houses, and if Strābo, who visited Rome in the reign of Tibērius, should accompany us to the Capitol to-day, he would hardly recognize the *Campus Martius* which he described so vividly. Of all the splendors which he saw, the Panthē'on alone has been completely preserved.

Yet that would well repay a visit to Rome:

"Simple, erect, severe, austere, sublime—
Shrine of all saints and temple of all gods,

PANTHEON IN ITS PRESENT CONDITION.

  * * * * * spared and bless'd by time,
   Looking tranquillity, while falls or nods
  Arch, empire, each thing round thee, and man plods
   His way through thorns to ashes—glorious dome!
  Shalt thou not last? Time's scythe and tyrants' rods
   Shiver upon thee—sanctuary and home
  Of art and piety—Pantheon! Pride of Rome!"
        —Byron, Childe Harold.

 Hawthorne puts these words in the mouths of his characters:
"The world has nothing else like the Panthē'on. * * * The rust
and dinginess that have dimmed the precious marble on the walls;

INTERIOR OF PANTHEON.

the pavement, with its great squares and rounds of porphyry and granite, cracked crosswise and in a hundred directions, showing how roughly the troublesome ages have trampled here; the grey dome above, with its opening to the sky, as if Heaven were looking down into the interior of this place of worship, left unimpeded for prayers to ascend the more freely: all these things make an impression of solemnity, which St. Peter's itself fails to produce."

"It is very delightful, on a breezy day, to see the masses of white cloud float over the opening, and then the sunshine fall through it again, fitfully, as it does now. Would it be any wonder if we were to see angels hovering there, partly in and partly out, with genial, heavenly faces, not intercepting the light, but transmuting it into beautiful colors? Look at that broad golden beam—a sloping cataract of sunlight—which comes down from the aperture, and rests upon the shrine, at the right hand of the entrance."—*Marble Faun.*

As the soil has acquired such depth, we do not notice that the Pantheon was originally above its level and was reached by a flight of five steps. The building consists of a portico 110 feet long by 44 feet deep, which is supported by sixteen noble Corinthian columns of granite, 36 feet in height (see initial letter), and a rotunda 143 feet in diameter, covered by a dome. An aperture 28 feet in diameter admits the light from above.

Narrow and crooked streets traverse this quarter, now densely covered with houses, and lead us to the foot of the *Campidoglio*, as the Cap'itoline Hill (*Mons Capitolinus*) is now called.

In the earliest times the rock projected abruptly into the *Campus Martius*. But in the time of Sulla permission was given to build on the Capitoline, and it was not long before the hill contained, besides its temples, a number of private houses. This explains how, in the year 69 A. D., the soldiers of Vitel'lius could press forward protected by the houses and ascend the hill on which the Temple of Jupiter had been built.

EQUESTRIAN STATUE OF MARCUS AURELIUS.

During the middle ages, not only the private houses but also the temples of the hill, the true monuments of ancient Roman power, fell into ruins; and then, over these ruins in later times, new streets were opened to this sacred height.

By the middle one of these roads, which was constructed by Michael Angelo, we can reach the summit most easily, as it has a gradual ascent. The younger ones among you will, no doubt, first hasten toward the shrubbery on the left, for there a couple of wolves are running impatiently hither and thither in a narrow cage. I need hardly tell you that it is only in thankful remembrance of that good-natured she-wolf, who is said to have suckled the founders of the city, that these innocent descendants have been condemned to a tedious imprisonment.

At first view, you will all think the Capitol has entirely changed its ancient form. But it has merely assumed a modern garb.

The present Capitoline Square, which is surrounded on three sides by modern buildings, and in whose centre stands the antique equestrian statue of Marcus Aurē'lius, has existed only since the sixteenth century. There is an interesting popular belief about this statue, which was originally gilded. It is fancied that it is turning into gold!

That there was originally a valley here is still plainly seen from the fact that steps lead from the square, right and left, to the two summits of the hill.

The southwestern of these summits the ancients called *Capitō'lium*, and the northeastern *Arx*, or the citadel. Between them, on the spot which, in the time of Livy, was still inclosed on

PLAN OF CAPITOLINE HILL.

account of its sanctity, Romulus is said to have opened his place of refuge for outlaws (*Asylum*). In this hollow, in very early times, was worshipped, between two groves, the god *Ve'jovis*.   To the sanctuary of this god the homeless, who were to people the young city of Romulus, were allowed to flee to make expiation, and then, cleansed from all past crimes, to pass through the gate of the Palatine city (*Roma Quadrata*).   There is no tradition of another temple between these hills.   Perhaps the awe inspired by the stern god *Vejovis*, who once demanded even human blood for atonement, was so great that they did not venture to hem in his jurisdiction by other buildings.   Besides, it was not easy to build on the slopes, while either of these two heights was a far more beautiful and prominent site for a temple.

You remember that Tarquinius Superbus, after the capture of Gabii, directed his attention to the arts of peace, and, above all, that he built on the Tarpe'ian Rock the Temple of Jupiter, which had been vowed by his father.   Livy, in the passage in which he describes this (I. 53–55), designates the whole southwestern part of the Capitoline Hill as *Rupes Tarpē'iae ;* but, in a narrower sense, the rock is a steep precipice toward the south,

> "Fittest goal of treason's race,
>   The promontory whence the traitor's leap
>   Cured all ambition."—*Byron.*

LIVY.

" One Tarpe'ius was governor of the citadel, whose daughter, Tarpe'ia by name, going forth from the walls to fetch water for a sacrifice, took money from the king that she should receive certain of the soldiers within the citadel; but when they had been so received, the men cast their shields upon her, slaying her with the weight of them.   This they did either that they might be thought to have taken the place by force, or that they judged it to be well that no faith should be kept with traitors! Some also tell this tale, that the Sā'bīnes wore great bracelets of gold on their left arms, and on their left hands fair rings with precious stones therein, and that when the maiden covenanted with them that she should have for a reward that which they carried in their left hands, they cast their shields upon her."—*Church.*

This place, where the first traitress of Rome received her reward from the mocking enemy, and whence afterwards perjurers, thieving slaves, and those accused of high treason were hurled down, has now lost its terrors. It is no longer separated from the rest of the Capitoline Hill by a wall; the trembling culprit is no longer led through the " poor sinners' " gate.

To be sure, the hill has undergone many changes in the course of time through landslides, so that no one can say definitely " This or that abrupt abyss was the grave of the transgressors." But this much, at any rate, is certain, that the ill-reputed place lay on this side of the hill.

For once, while, to steal the state treasures which were preserved in the Temple of Săt'urn, at the upper end of the Forum, burglars were busy with their crow-bars at its firm foundation ; their blows re-echoed from the perpendicular wall of the Tarpeian Rock near by, and thus betrayed the presence of the incautious robbers.

Livy, in his account of the founding of the Temple of Jupiter, has already informed you where to look for that largest and most sacred temple of Rome. But at present we need no longer rely on the written account alone ; the stones have spoken louder and more intelligibly than human tongues.

In the rebuilding operations on the southern side of the Capitoline Hill, during the years 1875–'78, the foundation walls of the old Temple of the Tarquins were brought to light.

The great age of these ruins is fully attested by the material of which they are composed, and the manner in which it was used; and the fact of their belonging to that temple is proved beyond all doubt by their position and mass.

On this spot, then, between his two companions, Juno and Miner'va, was enthroned the omnipotent Roman god of empire, who made this, his temple-house, the capitol of the world.

THE EMPORIUM.

TEMPLE OF JUPITER CAPITOLINUS.

THE TIBER.

Here the young Romans offered sacrifices upon laying aside the dress of boyhood (the *toga praetexta*); here the consuls entered on the duties of their office; hither the victorious generals, after having been borne in triumph through the city, directed their steps to express their gratitude in the temple of their mighty god.

> "The Tarpeian rock, the citadel
> Of great and glorious Rome, queen of the earth,
> So far renowned and with the spoils enriched
> Of nations."   —*Milton.*

And not only mortals sought here safety and deliverance, but even celestials, with their sanctuaries, altars and chapels, joined themselves closely to the supreme deity—"Father of gods and king of men."

This temple, which the Etruscans had helped the Romans to build, just as the Phœni'cians before had helped the Jews to build their temple, was burned down during the civil wars of Marius and Sulla. But through the provision of Sulla and his friend Căt'ulus, it was rebuilt on the old site even more splendidly than before; and, the more Greek art came into favor in Rome, the more richly was the temple adorned with statuary.

SULLA.

Twice again Jupiter was obliged to behold a sudden and violent destruction of his abode. Tac'itus tells, in his "Histories" (III., 71), and with the greatest indignation, how the Capitol was destroyed in the most shameful manner by the soldiers of Vitellius. Sabínus, the brother and general of Vespā'sian, caused the statues, although they were the monuments of his ancestors, to be torn down, that he might use them to barricade the principal entrance. The enemy, however, by side paths, penetrated the inclosure of the temple; the fire seized upon the colonnades; the wooden gable-ends of the temple fed the flames, and the Capitol was burned down ("*clausis foribus, indefensum et indireptum*"). Vespasian rebuilt the temple, but scarcely was it completed when it a third time sank in ashes during the great fire in the reign of Titus.

Under Domi'tian it was rebuilt with more splendor than before; but this very splendor was the ruin of the temple, for it invited the greedy barbarians.

The temple of the Roman State hastened inevitably toward its destruction, as the bonds of the empire became relaxed; and, when the master of the house himself, the mightiest Olympian, was dethroned, his temple fell into neglect and ruin.

As if to commemorate the overthrow of heathenism, there stands now on the northern and highest summit of the Capitoline Hill, on the Roman *Arx*, a Christian church, dedicated to the Virgin Mary. It stands on the very spot where the Romans, in the fourth century B. C., erected a temple to Juno Mone'ta. Why she was called *Moneta*, even Cicero could no longer explain with certainty. She is said, on one occasion, while a pestilence was raging in the city, to have caused her voice to be heard from the citadel, and by her good advice or admonition to have relieved the distress of the citizens.

Such stories, however, were only resorted to in order to account in an easy way for the name of the goddess, which was already in existence. *Moneta* has the same root as *moneo* (advise) and *mens* (mind), and signifies the reflecting or thinking one. Under this name the goddess, no doubt, was worshipped on this hill in very early times, just as Jupiter Stā'tor was worshipped on the Palatine—the powerful god on the one hill, the wise goddess on the other.

This hill was chosen for the citadel because it greatly exceeded in height the southern summit of the Capitoline.

Within the fortification there was, of course, no room for several large temples; and yet for convenience they united with the Temple of Juno, which was so securely situated, the arrangements for coining—a circumstance which has given the word *moneta* the meaning *mint*. The fact that the augur especially consulted (*augurac'ulum*) the gods on this hill, from which there is an extensive view across the Forum as far as the Cælian Hill, is learned from Livy, where he gives an account (I., 18) of the accession to the throne of the pious Numa. It is possible that this *auguraculum* was also a relic of the prehistoric worship of the queen of heaven on this citadel.

Now, if we descend from the Capitoline by the shortest way to the *Forum Romā'num*, we shall have on our right hand the present *Palazzo del Senato're*, erected on the site of the Roman archives, or *Tabulā'rium*. This *Tabularium* was built after the plans of Sulla and Catulus, the latter of whom had restored the Temple of Jupiter. It connected both summits of the Capitoline. A covered colon-nade afforded an easy communication from the one to the other, and a stairway led up to the building, and on through to the ancient *Asylum*. At present, the entrances to the forum are walled up, and we will therefore content ourselves to-day with admiring from without the "ancient and honorable" blocks of tufa, and the arches of the *Tabularium*. But you will be much more charmed by the view which we shall have on our way of the forum (*Forum Romanum*).

This most beautiful and animated square of ancient Rome now lies in silent sorrow, and only the ruins of its former grandeur remain. Once so infinitely rich, it has now become a beggar, and excites our compassion by its threadbare garments. Only the proud remembrance of its youth remains. A wonderful thing is this *Forum Romanum*. If we contemplate it from our present ele-vation, and, as if riveted to the ground, find that we cannot turn our eyes from it, suddenly the solitude beneath us will become alive. Mighty temples arise from the depth before our rapt gaze, and triumphal arches again span the sacred street.

Now the people, also, come back to our view. Silently and gravely the priests are ascending the steps of the lofty temples; the business-man hastens to the stall of the money-changer, and is soon in animated conversation with the greedy banker. Thought-less idlers are sauntering about in the paved square, discussing with important air the events of the day. But suddenly everybody turns toward the sacred street (*Via Sacra*). The Commander-in-chief of the Army (*Imperā'tor*), returning home in triumph, is

Temple of Castor.

THE FORUM IN FESTAL ATTIRE.

approaching from the eastern hills. The procession is headed by the Senate, who, in festal robes, have received the conqueror and his army at the gate of the city. Next come the trumpeters. Behind these are creaking the wagons laden with booty; and here and there among them are seen, towering up boastfully, the litters with the more precious pieces of booty carried on the shoulders of sturdy men.

As the wagons approach the crowd, every man stretches his neck to read, from the tablets carried on high, what province has been subdued, how much booty has been taken, and to whom the costly weapons and coats-of-arms had formerly belonged. The noisy crowd becomes more silent on the approach of the priests, the bullock adorned with white ribbons in their midst; but loud shouts of joy break forth to greet the conqueror as he proceeds on his way to the Capitol, clad in an embroidered tōga, and borne upon a triumphal chariot, which is adorned with ivory, and drawn by four horses. Joy and pride shine in the victor's face, because he is permitted to enter his native city with such honor, surrounded by his sons, and followed by his victorious soldiers.

The procession is gone, the crowd has dispersed, and we awake from our dream.

We now hasten down the hill and take a look at the so-called Mam'ertine prison (*Carcer*). This, as is well known, is the name of the Roman state prison. The upper part is said to have been built by Ancus Marcius, and Servius Tullius is supposed to have added the lower, subterranean part. At present, the whole is covered by a small church, at the entrance of which the Apostles Peter and Paul are represented in rude frescoes languishing behind the bars of the prison. A modern stairway leads us down into the upper story of the prison. This is a chamber, inclosed by thick walls, which originally was accessible only by means of a rectangular opening in the ceiling.

Of this Dickens says: "There is an upper chamber in the Mamertine prisons, over what is said to have been—and very pos-

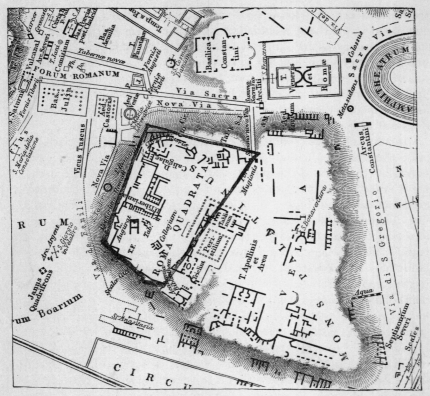

PLAN OF FORUM AND PALATINE.

sibly may have been—the dungeon of St. Peter. The chamber is
now fitted up as an oratory, dedicated to that saint; and it lives, as
a distinct and separate place, in my recollection, too. It is very
small and low-roofed; and the dread and gloom of the ponderous,
obdurate old prison are on it, as if they had come up in a dark mist
through the floor. Hanging on the walls, among the clustered
votive offerings, are objects at once strangely in keeping and
strangely at variance with the place—rusty daggers, knives, pistols,
clubs, divers instruments of violence and murder, brought here,

fresh from use, and hung up to propitiate offended heaven, as if the blood upon them would drain off in consecrated air and have no voice to cry with.   It is all so silent and so close and tomb-like, and the dungeons below are so black and stealthy and stagnant and naked that this little dark spot becomes a dream within a dream ; and in the vision of great churches which come rolling past me like a sea, it is a small wave by itself that melts into no other wave, and does not flow on with the rest."

In this cell were confined the great criminals, such as parricides and traitors, for whom the ordinary prisons were not severe enough.   (Sallust, in the passage in which he speaks of the punishment inflicted on the associates of Catiline, calls this chamber a "*camera fornicibus vincta.*")   But far more dreaded was the cellar-like dungeon underneath : ("*Incultu, tenebris, odore foeda atque terribilis ejus facies est.*")   Of this the stones of the walls are so laid as to form a dome, each row or layer projecting a little over the one below it.   The keystone of the dome has been taken out, in order to give connection with the upper chamber.   As there is, right beneath this opening, a well, it is evident that this ancient vault was built to guard the well.   The vault was called *Tullia'num*, a name which signifies nothing else than " House of the Well," and denotes here the well belonging to the *Arx*.   But since this traditional name recalled the third King of Rome, Tullus Hostilius, it was natural to ascribe to that opulent ruler the construction of this as well as of the so-called *Curia Hostil'ia*.   But, even if this building had been originally a prison, it would be difficult to say why it was built exactly over a well.   Tradition has it that so great was the impression made by the preaching of Peter and Paul that the two jailers and forty-seven prisoners were converted, and, that they might immediately be baptized, God caused this well to burst forth !   From the time of Ancus Marcius it may have been used as a prison, especially since on account of the building placed above it it had become a dark and damp hole.   Only those condemned to death, however, were thrust into this dungeon.

Here Jugur'tha was starved to death. He had been dragged along in the triumphal procession of Marius, and the Roman plebs had exulted because the crafty Numidian prince had been conquered by Marius, himself of plebe'ian birth. Hardly has Jugurtha been led away toward the prison from the triumphal procession at the end of the *Via Sacra*, when the infuriated multitude rush upon him. In spite of the guards he is struck, his clothes are torn, and his golden earrings, and with them the flaps of his ears, are wrenched off. And so, bleeding and almost naked, he has arrived at the prison. But these executioners have no compassion ; he is thrust down into the horrible dungeon below. Well might the cold chills run over him as he exclaimed, "By Hercules, how cold your bath is !"

> " The victor, springing from his seat,
>   Went up, and, kneeling as in fervent prayer,
>   Entered the Capitol. But what are they
>   Who at the foot withdraw, a mournful train
>   In fetters ? And who, yet incredulous,
>   Now gazing wildly round, now on his sons,
>   On those so young, well pleased with all they see,
>   Staggers along, the last ? They are the fallen,
>   Those who were spared to grace the chariot-wheels ;
>   And there they parted, where the road divides,
>   The victor and the vanquished—there withdrew ;
>   He to the festal board, and they to die."   —*Rogers's Italy.*

To this prison, also, Catiline's fellow-conspirators, who had remained behind in the city after the departure of their leader, were brought, condemned to death in spite of the opposition of Cæsar. Cicero himself conducted Lentulus, who had lived in lax custody on the Palatine Hill, across the forum to the prison ; the rest were led by the prætors. They, also, were let down into the gloomy dungeon, but a speedy death put an end to their lives— the executioners (*Vindices rerum capitalium*), strangled them.

But I see you have come to feel quite uncomfortable in this *Carcer*, and I will, therefore, take you out into the open air again.

THE ARCH OF SEVERUS, WEST SIDE, AS TO-DAY.

To be sure, if it were the ancient street into which we were going, a horrible sight might yet meet our eyes. For hard by the *Carcer* was the so-called "stairway of groans" (*Scalae gemonianae*), on which the bodies of executed criminals were exposed, so that the whole Roman forum might see them, and the sight inspire great but wholesome horror ("*magno cum horrore.*") It was here that the miserable Vitellius fell in his vain flight. In order to reach the forum from this side, we must descend a temporary flight of wooden stairs. Turning to the right now, we look through the middle one of the three triumphal portals of the arch (*Arcus triumphalis*) of Septimius Sevĕ'rus. This somewhat clumsy edifice was erected in the year 203 A. D., to commemorate the victories of this emperor

CARACALLA.

over the Parthians. The large middle archway communicates with each of the smaller ones by still smaller arches inside. It was probably built over a street. It stands so high above the original level of the forum that the side arches had to be reached by seven steps. When still adorned with all its decorations it must, it is true, have been much finer. (Above the main passage there was a long inscription, in metal letters, rehearsing the achievements of the imperial family. (In the fourth line we now read, "OPTIMIS FORTISSIMISQUE PRINCIPIBUS." But originally, as we may conclude from the marks left of the fastenings of the letters, it must have read, " P. SEPTIMIO GETAE NOBILISSIMO CAESARI OPT.")

But when, after his father's death, Caracalla had glutted his hatred of his brother Geta, by making away with him, he caused his odious name to be removed from this monument of victory, on the pretense that it was too shocking to be continually reminded of his dead brother.) Trophies were fastened to the right and left of the inscription, and above the arch there stood a gilded chariot drawn by six horses (*Currus sejugis*), seemingly in triumphant course, in which was the emperor, crowned by a *Victoria.* Close to the triumphal chariot marched Caracalla and Geta, whom their father had permitted to share alike the glory of the house. At the corners of the top, at present so bare, were placed equestrian statues, so that the whole may well have produced an imposing impression.

We now enter the middle portal of the arch to escape the Italian November sun, and have before us the colossal substructure of the Temple of Concord (*Templum Concordiae*). The earliest building was vowed 367 B. C. by Camillus the Dictator, in gratitude for the restoration of union of the Patricians and Plebeians. After Camillus's death it was constructed by the Senate and people. But, by such a nod of Nemesis as caused the first battle of our revolution to be fought at Concord, this temple, immediately after the slaughter of Caius Gracchus and 3,000 of his followers, was dedicated by their butcher, Opimius, to Concord!! Falling into decay, it was renovated and enlarged by Tiberius, in compliance with Augustus's wish. Even in the times of the Republic it was a spacious temple, as the Senate oftentimes assembled here. The splendor of the pillars, indeed, has passed away, but still we distinctly make out stairs ascending in terraces and leading to an ante-structure, behind which the broad temple projected on both sides.

In it the Senate had convened in crowded assembly on that memorable 3d of December, when Cicero held in his hand the evidence against the Catilinarian conspirators, obtained through the ambassadors of the Allöb'roges. The conference lasted until evening. Impatiently the populace streamed up and down before the stairs of the temple, when at last the Consul, emerging from the mysterious interior (*cella*) of the temple, informed the apprehensive citizens (*Quiri'tes*) that he had removed the impending

MARCUS TULLIUS CICERO.

danger. "But not I myself have accomplished this—that were saying too much—nay, Jove on high hath withstood. He it is that desired to see saved his capitol, these temples here—ay, the entire city, and all of you."

Imagine for a moment that, with the Roman citizens, you had been fearing for your lives and property; that you had already seen in your minds the houses of the city in flames: would not that man whose majestic form shone down from above into the dusk of evening like that of a god, who so calmly, and yet inspired with the

I. Bühmann, 1882

WEST END FORUM IN TIME OF DOMITIAN.

Basilica.   Temple of Jupiter.   T. Vespasian.   Tabularium.   T. Concord.
                 T. Saturn

joy of victory, was speaking to you—would not he necessarily appear to you a savior, a father of his fatherland (*Pater patriæ*)? Probably you would not have suffered yourselves to be sent home with soothing words; you, too, as brave *quirites*, would have lighted torches and formed an escort of honor for the deliverer of the city.

Just at the side of the left-hand portal there has been brought to light a cone-shaped brick structure, which evidently served as

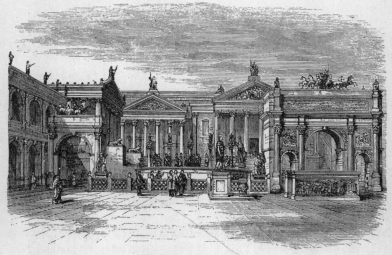

WEST FORUM, TIME OF SEVERUS.

a basis for something. Probably the *Umbili′cus*, an imitation of the Delphic Omphalos (Ὀμφαλός), stood in this place. (The Ὀμφαλός was a white stone in the form of a truncated cone, standing near Apollo's altar, and considered by the Greeks as the centre of the world.) The Roman Emperor, in order that the Romans might become cognizant of their high position in the world, located the centre of his empire at the *Umbili′cus*, by which the people daily passed.

Below the Temple of Saturn stood the golden milestone (*Milli-ā'rium Aureum*), erected by Augustus in 25 B. C. Not of stone, but of gilt bronze, it gleamed forth from its elevated standpoint over the entire forum.   The names and distances of the different gates of the city were marked upon it, while the centre itself of the empire was represented by the *umbilicus*.

Upon the platform (the *Graecostasis*), erected between these two foreign ambassadors, during the empire, used to listen to the orations addressed to the people from the speakers' platform lying directly in front.

The *Graeco'stasis* was built of immense blocks of tufa with portions of harder stone—an evidence of early construction. It was also embellished with marble. You must not confound the most ancient *Rostra* with the *Rostra* here. The former stood on the *Comitium*, to the north of the forum.

> " The forum, where the immortal accents glow,
>   And still the eloquent air breathes—burns with Cicero."—*Byron.*

But that place had long since become too small for the public meetings, and Augustus therefore removed the *Rostra* to the western end of the forum, where the orators had a vast expanse before them.

The *Via Sacra* terminates at the *Milliā'rium Aureum*, to be continued by the only highway leading to the Capitoline Hill—*i. e.*, the *Clīvus Capitolī'nus*. This highway was among the first in Rome to be paved, 174 B. C.

If we follow this ancient road, we have, to the left, one of the most stupendous ruins, situated at the upper end of the forum. I mean the substructure cf Saturn's Temple, with its eight Ionic columns still standing. These, as well as the entire decorations, date back to a restoration that was undertaken in the third century of the Christian era. The lower part of the temple, as is well known, was used for the treasury. Its lofty and firm walls are doubtless of great antiquity. Tradition ascribes this edifice, and

RUINS.   TEMPLE OF SATURN.   TEMPLE OF VESPASIAN.

the introduction of the festivities in honor of the god Saturn
(*Saturnā'lia*) to Tullus Hostílius. Others say that Tarquinius
Superbus erected it. It was probably begun under the kings,
completed during the republic, and consecrated by the first Dictator
of Rome, Títus Lartius, in 501 B. C.

Opposite the high stairway, which led to the Temple of Saturn,
a small temple was built by Domitian, in honor of Vespasian. As
there was also placed in it an image of Titus, the people were

RUINS.

Area of Dii Consentes.   Temple of Vespasian.

wont to call it after the two Flavii (Vespasian and Titus). Of the inscription there remain only the letters ESTITVER, which must be read as a part of RESTITVERVNT ("they restored"). These relate to the restoration of the sanctuary by Septimius Severus and Caracalla.

The front of the temple, which once was adorned by six columns of Carrara marble, faces the forum. Its sides, which were supported each by eleven pillars, run parallel with the Concordia Temple. The back rests on the *Tabularium*. Three columns are still standing at the right hand front corner. They support part of the molding adorned with the heads of oxen and with sacrificial implements. When, in the beginning of this century, an attempt was made to excavate them to their full length, the foundation proved to be too frail for the pillars. After it had been strengthened, they were again put up, and with great pains and trouble the molding was restored from the fragments found.

Passing by this small temple, several stairs conduct us down from the *Clivus* to a row of chambers. Both these and those lying above served as offices for the scribes and town-criers of the Ædiles. Before these chambers a narrow portico extends, surrounding a small space at the southern side, which was consecrated to the twelve chief Olympic gods (*Dii Consentes*). Even though the structure, of which these ruins remain, is of the latest times, it may yet be concluded, from a passage of the second Philippic, that already in the days of Cicero the Curulian Ædiles had their rooms here.

Antonius had charged the consul with having the whole of the *Clivus Capitolinus* occupied by armed slaves in the year 63 B. C., while that decisive session in the Concordia Temple was going on. This charge is thus refuted by Cicero, in just indignation : "O wretched fellow, whether these proceedings are unknown to you—you know, indeed, nothing that is good—or if they are known, since you speak so impudently in the presence of such men ! *Quis enim eques Romanus, quis praeter te adulescens nobilis, quis ullius ordinis, qui se*

civem esse meminisset, cum senatus in hoc templo esset in Clivo Capito-
lino non fuit ? Who in those days would have been loath to have his
name enrolled as one ready to guard with arms the fatherland's weal?
Ay, there were not scribes
enough ; the tablets suf-
ficed not for recording the
names of those that pre-
sented themselves."

Since at the above-
mentioned area of the
twelve chief deities or
advising gods (*Dii Consen-*
tes) the new street is built
over the old, we must here
turn ; on our way back
we look for awhile at the
workmen, who, just under
the road which leads
obliquely across the
forum, are bringing to
light remains of walls
dating from the Middle
Ages, and then digging
down to the forum itself.
In order to fairly judge

MARCUS ANTONIUS.

of the dimensions of the forum, we must imagine the pillar
removed, which in the seventh century was erected in honor of the
Byzantine Emperor Phocas, for with its extensive foundation it fills
up a good part of the western end.

The forum, laid with limestone flags, has the form of a trapezium,
the shortest side of which forms the east border. On the north
side, the rubbish-heap reaches even yet to a height of several
metres. And it is only recently that they have begun to lay bare
here the ancient soil. There still repose, in the deep sleep of the cen-

COLUMN OF PHOCAS.   TEMPLE OF SATURN.   OFFICES.   T. VESPASIAN.

turies, the most important public buildings of the Romans; there, as has already been said, lay the voting-place of the Roman people, the Comitium, together with the City Hall; there stood the speakers' platform of the republic; there was built the first court of justice, which was shortly followed by a second and grander one. Perhaps it will be possible, at no distant day, to follow out more distinctly the remains of these foundations. The houses which are still standing over them have been purchased by the Italian Government, and look as sombre and neglected as if they had a premonition of their speedy destruction

From the forum the square blocks of stone, which project from the embankment of the modern street, can be examined to better advantage. They served as foundations to the speakers' platform of the imperial period. This must have been very spacious. The

Rostra consisted of a nearly rectangular platform, 75 feet by 44, built of tufa. The surface was divided by pillars into squares, and bore the speakers' platform. The front of the speakers' platform was faced with green marble, and here the ship-beaks (*rostra*), were fastened in two rows, nineteen in one, twenty in the other. The *Rostra* was adorned with statues of the ambassadors who had died when away from Rome, and in front were the tables of the laws. Augustus not only caused the insignia of the republican platform, the ships' beaks of Antium, to be attached to the new one, but he also brought here

TRAJAN.

all the marble statues and decorations which the people had erected there to men of renown. Many a piece, weak with age, had then to be replaced, as also the inscription on the column in honor of Gaius Duillius, the fragments of which have been dug up here.

Only one antique art-work is preserved intact in the forum.

That is the so-called Barriers of marble.   The two pieces, each five metres long, stand opposite each other, as if they formed the railing of a narrow bridge.   On the inside of each three stately sacrificial beasts—boar, sheep and bullock—are making their last journey. On the outer sides the Emperor Tra′jan is represented, as he proclaims in the forum his gift for the education of poor children, and as he orders the lists of unpaid taxes to be burned.

Whether these remarkable stones were originally erected here, and what end they served, are questions that cannot be answered

TRAJAN BURNING THE TAX LISTS.

Basilica Julia.   Temple of Saturn.   Temple of Vespas.   Rostra.   T. Concord.

with certainty.   It is certain that from the background of the scenes depicted on them we have received great help in restoring the forum. We can apply the term barriers with greater certainty to the eight bulky, square structures along the south side, for to them were fastened the rope and the rows of boards by which the place was enclosed during the assemblies.

In old times this city square had a very different appearance,

VIRGINIA AT PLAY.

being surrounded on all sides by shabby booths.   The butchers had their shops ("*taber'næ*") here, which certainly did not make the ground cleaner, nor the air purer.   Next door clinked the coins of the money-changers; and in this noisy neighborhood were also schoolrooms, or, as the Romans called them, "*ludi puerorum.*" How often the children must have stopped at those shops; and among the butchers, certainly they must have had their special friends!   It would be interesting to know if the Roman boys then could beg so winsomely for a Roman "penny" ("*as*"), as now for an Italian *soldo*.

Once the children, on their way to school, were greatly terrified. A servant of the dreaded decĕm'vir, Appius Claudius, seized and led away from them their playmate Virginia, and brought her before the neighboring tribunal of his patron, asserting that Virginia, as the daughter of one of his slaves, belonged to him.

" The city gates were opened : the forum, all alive
With buyers and with sellers, was humming like a hive.
Blithely on brass and timber the craftsman's stroke was ringing,
And blithely o'er her panniers the market-girl was singing,
And blithely young Virginia came smiling from her home :
Ah! wo for young Virginia, the sweetest maid in Rome !

WAX TABLETS.   STYLUS.

With her small tablets in her hand, and her satchel on her arm,
Forth she went bounding to the school, nor dreamed of shame or harm.
She crossed the forum shining with stalls in alleys gay,
And just had reached this very spot whereon I stand this day,
When up the varlet Marcus came ; not such as when erewhile
He crouched behind his patron's heels with the true client's smile :
He came with lowering forehead, swollen features, and clinched fist
And strode across Virginia's path, and caught her by the wrist.
Hard strove the frighted maiden, and screamed with look aghast ;
And at her scream from right and left the folk came running fast ;
The money-changer Crispus, with his thin silver hairs,
And Hanno from the stately booth glittering with Punic wares,

And the strong smith Muræna, grasping a half-forged brand,
And Volero the flesher, his cleaver in his hand.
All came in wrath and wonder; for all knew that fair child;
And, as she passed them twice a day, all kissed their hands and smiled.
And the strong smith Muræna gave Marcus such a blow,
The caitiff reeled three paces back, and let the maiden go.
Yet glared he fiercely round him, and growled in harsh, fell tone.
' She 's mine, and I will have her, I seek but for mine own :
She is my slave, born in my house, and stolen away and sold
The year of the sore sickness, ere she was twelve hours old.
'T was in the sad September, the month of wail and fright,
Two augurs were borne forth that morn ; the consul died ere night.
I wait on Appius Claudius ; I waited on his sire ;
Let him who works the client wrong, beware the patron's ire.'
So spake the varlet Marcus ; and dread and silence came
On all the people at the sound of the great Claudian name."

—Macaulay.

But a still more fearful experience awaited them on the morrow.
As early as daybreak the whole body of the citizens stood in the
forum in anxious curiosity, for on that day the fate of the maiden
was to be decided. Virginius, also, who had been brought in hot
haste from the neighboring camp, came long before the beginning
of the trial, and sought by his grief to arouse the sympathy of the
by-standers. He stepped up to different individuals, pressed their
hands, and spoke to them in a loud voice, so that all might hear,
of the danger which threatened them too, if they would not protect
him. Of the trial itself, not every word reached the ears of the
listening boys, but they soon saw that something altogether out
of the common run must follow the violent altercation between the
judge and the defendant.

Suddenly they heard Appius cry with a voice of thunder:
"Lic'tor, disperse the crowd and allow the master to seize his
slave." (" *Lictor, summove turbam et da viam domino ad prendendum
manicipium.*") Great and small scattered when it was seen that the
servants of the state were in earnest to fulfil the command of
their master. Virginius alone preserved his composure. With

seeming calmness, he begged of the decemvirs permission to speak a word or two of farewell to his daughter.

Then, leading Virginia a little way apart from the crowd to the butchers' shops, which lay near by the *Comitium*, he snatched up a knife and plunged it into his daughter's heart with the words: "Thus only, my child, can I save thee for freedom." But turning to the tribunal, he cried: "Thee, Appius, and thy life by this blood I curse!" ("*Te, Appi, tuumque caput sanguine hoc consecro!*") Then he rushed forth, breaking his way through the midst of the lictors, to arouse his comrades in the camp to take vengeance upon the tyrants who had driven him to so terrible a deed.

"Straightway Virginius led the maid a little space aside,
To where the reeking shamble stood, piled up with horn and hide.
Close to yon low dark archway, where, in crimson flood,
Leaps down to the great sewer the gurgling stream of blood.
Hard by, a flesher on a block had laid his whittle down;
Virginius caught the whittle up, and hid it in his gown.
And then his eyes grew very dim, and his throat began to swell,
And in a hoarse, changed voice, he spake, 'Farewell, sweet child, farewell!
Oh! how I loved my darling! Though stern I sometimes be,
To thee, thou knowest, I was not so. Who could be so to thee?
And how my darling loved me! How glad she was to hear
My footsteps on the threshold, when I came back last year!
And how she danced with pleasure to see my civic crown,
And took my sword, and hung it up, and brought me forth my gown!
Now, all these things are over—yes, all thy pretty ways,
Thy needle-work, thy prattle, thy snatches of old lays;
And none will grieve when I go forth, or smile when I return,
Or watch beside the old man's bed, or weep upon his urn.
The house that was the happiest within the Roman walls,
The house that envied not the wealth of Capua's marble halls,
Now, for the brightness of thy smile, must have eternal gloom,
And for the music of thy voice, the silence of the tomb.
                                        —*Macaulay.*

The place in which such exciting scenes could be enacted was certainly not a favorable place for schools, and the Romans did well to put them at a distance. The stalls of the fishermen also had to

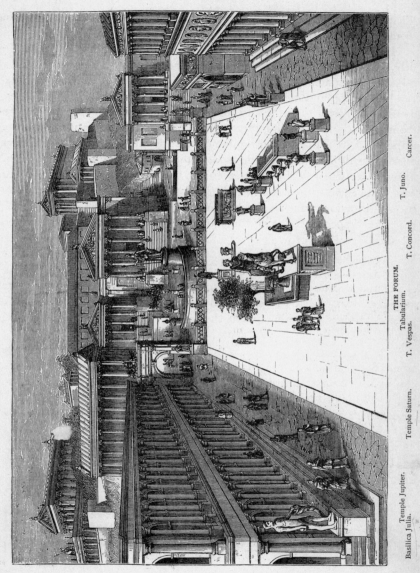

THE FORUM.

Basilica Julia. Temple Jupiter. Temple Saturn. T. Vespas. Tabularium. T. Concord. T. Juno. Carcer.

disappear, as more attention was given to the beautifying of the square; only the bankers might remain.

Instead of the low shops the elegant pillared halls of the Basíl'-icas, built after the Greek model, now adorned the forum. Cæsar laid the foundation for the most beautiful at the south side; Augustus built it up and called it after his uncle, *Basilica Julia*. It was separated from the gathering place of the people by the *Via Sacra*, from which a few steps led up to the portico: if you entered at the upper end, you needed to mount only three steps; but at the lower end, seven. This riddle would be difficult to solve if you did not know that the surface of the forum sinks somewhat toward the east, while the top of the foundation of the Basilica is level. The roomy interior was used for the transactions of the courts, was capable of accommodating four law courts consisting of 180 jurymen (*judices*), and the crowds of spectators, and could be shut off from the surrounding porches.

In these, and upon the steps, the children and wandering musicians moved about, as in the Rome of to-day they lounge upon the church steps. That these not only chatted and slept there, but also played eagerly, is evident from the many gaming boards which are scratched on the marble slabs and pavement.

If we step down to the *Via Sacra*, at the east of the Basilica, we are but a few paces from the ascent to the temple of Castor and Pollux. The foundation is well preserved, and also a part of the mosaic floor of the *cella*, but only three columns are standing on the side, which are now bound together with iron bars. Certainly they are old enough to be supported, for they date from the time of Tiberius, who rebuilt this temple after a fire.

It was founded by the young republic in honor of the two knightly youths who, in the fight at Lake Regillus, had helped in a wonderful manner to gain a great victory.

> " So like they were, no mortal might one from other know:
> White as snow their armor was: their steeds were white as snow.
> Never on earthly anvil did such rare armor gleam;

RUINS.

Temple of Castor and Pollux.   Temple Saturn.

And never did such gallant steeds drink of an earthly stream.
And all who saw them trembled, and pale grew every cheek;
And Aulus, the Dictator, scarce gathered voice to speak.
'Say, by what name men call you?   What city is your home?
And wherefore ride ye in such guise before the ranks of Rome?'
'By many names men call us; in many lands we dwell:
Well Samothracia knows us: Cyrē'nè knows us well.
Our house in gay Tarentum is hung each morn with flowers:
High o'er the masts of Syracuse our marble portal towers:
But by the proud Eurō'tas is our dear native home;
And for the right we come to fight before the ranks of Rome.'
So answered these strange horsemen, and each couched low his spear;
And forthwith all the ranks of Rome were bold and of good cheer:
And on the thirty armies came wonder and affright,
And Ardea wavered on the left, and Cora on the right.
'Rome to the charge!' cried Aulus; 'The foe begins to yield.
Charge for the hearth of Vesta!   Charge for the golden shield!
Let no man stop to plunder, but slay, and slay, and slay:
The gods who live forever are on our side to-day.' "

CASTOR AND POLLUX.

The temple was built on this spot because Castor and Pollux had suddenly appeared here after that battle, had announced the victory, and watered their sweating and thirsty horses in a little pool (the *Lacus Juturnae*). (Our illustrations are from coins, a *Quinā'rius* and a *Denā'rius*.)

CASTOR AND POLLUX AT THE SPRING.

"Since the first gleam of daylight, Sempronius had not ceased
To listen for the rushing of horse-hoofs from the east.
The mist of eve was rising, the sun was hastening down,
When he was aware of a princely pair fast pricking towards the town.
So like they were, man never saw twins so like before;
Red with gore their armor was, their steeds were red with gore.
'Hail to the great asylum! hail to the hill-tops seven!
Hail to the fire that burns for aye, and the shield that fell from heaven!
This day, by Lake Regillus, under the Porcian height,

All in the lands of Tusculum, was fought a glorious fight.
To-morrow your Dictator shall bring in triumph home
The spoils of thirty cities to deck the shrines of Rome!'
Then burst from the great concourse a shout that shook the towers,
And some ran north and some ran south, crying 'The day is ours!'
But on rode those strange horsemen, with slow and lordly pace;
And none who saw their bearing durst ask their name or race.
On rode they to the forum, while laurel-boughs and flowers,
From house-tops and from windows, fell on their crest in showers.
When they drew nigh to Vesta, they vaulted down amain,
And washed their horses in the well that springs by Vesta's fane.
And straight again they mounted, and rode to Vesta's door;
Then, like a blast, away they passed, and no man saw them more."

—*Macaulay.*

SOUTH-EAST FORUM.

Temple of Vesta.
Arch of Augustus.   Temple Divus Julius.   Temple of Castor.   Basilica.

The Temple of Castor and Pollux was so spacious that often the sessions of the Senate were held there, and the statesmen liked to address the people from the steps of the sanctuary. Julius Cæsar especially liked to talk here, and in remembrance of that, Augustus had a rostrum placed near the temple, which he built directly opposite it in honor of "*Divus Julius.*" The front of this rostrum was adorned with beaks of ships captured at Actium. Just beyond was the Arch of Augustus.

Face to face stood the ancient Republic and the young Empire, for on the further side of the square, below the Capitol, was the

Rostra, with trophies of the victories of the Republic ; on this side shone the evidences of the glory of the Julian family, who through their buildings always strove to draw the attention of the people more and more away from the ancient Republic.

On account of the erection of Cæsar's Temple, a rearrangement of this portion of the forum became necessary, which must have affected the direction of the street. At least

CAIUS JULIUS CÆSAR.

it is certain that the *Via Sacra* went beyond to the circular temple of Vesta, but the ruin of that building is generally pointed out at the east of the Temple of Castor and Pollux.

"Close to where the southern angle of the Temple of Castor stands back from the forum, stood the altar of *Aius Locu'tius,* in the open at the edge of the *Nova Via* (" new street "), really one of the oldest streets in Rome, and reminding us of the period when the *Via Sacra,* to which it found access behind the *Atrium Vestae* ("House of Vesta"), and the forum itself were newly in the boundary of the city. On the line of this *Nova Via* stands the lately discovered 'House of the Vestals,' between which and the Grove of Vesta on the slope of the Palatine it runs obliquely toward the southwest." "People abroad can not conceive the faintest idea of the impression which every one here felt in stepping over

TEMPLE OF DIVUS JULIUS.   TEMPLE OF CASTOR.   ARCH OF AUGUSTUS.   BASILICA.

the threshold of the *Atrium Vestae*, in entering those cloisters, the marble population of which is increasing in number and in importance every day. The noble, dignified portrait-statues of the *virgines vestales maximae* (chief vestal virgins) are there standing in long array, ready to welcome the visitors, and glad to have recovered possession of the house which, for eleven centuries, has been the witness of their joys and sorrows, the depository of their secrets, and from which they were brutally expelled in A. D. 394."

Now Horace meets us, as in his customary walk he comes down the *Via Sacra*. But to-day the poet, usually so cheerful, is in bad humor; for a disagreeable, persistent man, entirely unknown to him, has intruded himself upon him, wishes to become his friend, and asks in a very inquisitive way after Mæcē'nas. Horace has, indeed, already told him that he should not need his company, as he wishes to visit one of his acquaintances on the farther side of the Tiber. But the fib was of no avail, for the new friend will go so far as to let a summons to court be disregarded, if he may only accom-

QUINTUS HORATIUS FLACCUS.

pany the poet. Horace is in the greatest perplexity, and is besides very angry because the roguish Fuscus, whom he had secretly greeted as his deliverer, makes merry over him, and will not understand grimaces and winks, but hastens away with a very poor excuse.

The new friends have just reached the Temple of Vesta, and

Horace knows that he must endure the persistent man an hour longer, in case that bore succeeds in getting by the court-house (*Basilica*) unnoticed into the Tuscan quarter (*Vicus Tuscus*). Fortunately, just there the enemy of this deserter meets them, and drags him before the nearest tribunal. But Horace continues his walk, and laughs now himself over his misfortune. His gay spirits have returned, and let him find amends for the lost time by working out some charming verses, with which he will, at the earliest opportunity, relate his experience to a gay circle of friends.

Walking by chance in the Sacred Street, I, true to my habit,
Turned in my mind some trifles or other—absorbed in them wholly.
Hurrying toward me there came a man whom I knew by name only.
Seizing my hand, he exclaimed : " How are you, my dearest of fellows?"
" Well, sir, at present," I answered, "and all that you wish I crave also."
Now as he joins me I try to forestall him. "What did you wish, then ?"
" Wish ?   That you knew me indeed," replied he, " for I am accomplished."
" So much the greater your value," said I, and, longing to leave him,
Quickened my steps ; made pause now and then to whisper some trifle
Into the ear of my boy, while I felt a cold perspiration
E'en on my feet. " O happy Bolā′nus in being quick-tempered !"
Envying, thought I, the while the tiresome creature kept prattling,
Praising the streets and the city and saying whatever he thought of.
Seeing I gave him no answer, he said : " You are wretchedly pining,
I know, to desert me, but I shall hold on to the last. You can't do it.
I will accompany you as far as your errand may lead you."
—" Do not go out of your way. I call on a friend whom you know not,
Ill far over the Tiber, near the gardens of Cæsar."
—" I have nothing to do and not being lazy I 'll follow."
Droop, then, my suffering ears, like those of an obstinate donkey—
Burden too great for his back being finally fastened upon it.
Then says the fellow : " If really you knew me, you would not like Viscus
Or Varius better than me ; for who can write verses more swiftly ?
Who can more gracefully dance ? and my voice let Hermogenes envy.
Here was a chance of inquiring : " Have you a mother,—relations
Cherishing fondly your welfare ?"—" No, not a relative have I ·
All have been laid away." " Happy ones !" thought I, " but *I* am remaining.
Finish me ! Now comes the fate foretold by the old Sabine woman.
I was a boy when, the sacred urn being shaken, she chanted :

'Neither shall poison carry him off, nor enemy's weapon,
Nor pleurisy, no, nor a cough, nor gout, howe'er it may cripple.
Some time or other a *bore* will consume him.   So let him shun talkers
If he be prudent, when once he attains the stature of manhood.'"
Now we had reached the Temple of Vesta at nine in the morning.
He, as it chanced, was then due to appear in court as defendant.
Failing in this, he would thereby forfeit his bail or his lawsuit.
—" Were you my friend," he said, " you here would aid me a little."
—" O ! may I die if I can, or know aught of this jurisprudence !
Then I am hastening whither I told you."—" I hesitate," said he,
" Whether to give up *you* or my lawsuit."   " Me, sir, by all means ! "
" I will not," he said, beginning to walk on.   And I meekly follow.
Hard it is, truly, for any to struggle on with a victor.
" How do you stand," he resumed, " with Mæcenas, that man of sound judgment,
Highly select in his friendships ?—none has used riches more wisely.
Helper indeed you might have, who would be an obedient second,
Would you now only employ my services.   Why ; may I die, if,
Then you could not remove all rivals far from your pathway ! "
—" Modes there of living are not what you think them.   No house is purer,
Freer from all such abuses.   To me it is no inconvenience
That others are richer or wiser than I.   To each his allotment."
—" Wonders scarce credible these are."—" So it is notwithstanding."
—" Greater than ever my wish is that I, too, may share his acquaintance."
—" Wishing in your case is all.   With merit like yours you may gain it.
He is a man to be wheedled ; therefore he guards his approaches."
—" Not an occasion shall pass me.   I 'll gain the servants by presents.
Were I to-day shut out, I should not give up, but would watch and
Meet him at last in the streets.   Be sure I shall finally have him,
Nothing is gained in life without mighty effort by mortals."—
While he is talking in this way, Fuscus Aristius meets me,
Friend well beloved of mine, who knows perfectly this fellow's habits.
Stopping we ask and we answer : " Whence do you come ? "—" Whither go you ?"
Clutching, I pinch his insensible arms, while nodding and winking
That he may release me from torture.   He, laughing with mischievous humor
Seems not to notice my hints.   My wrath, in the meantime, is boiling.
—" Surely you said that you wished to tell me something in private."
—" Yes, I distinctly remember.   I 'll say it on better occasion.
This is the thirtieth Sabbath.   You wish to scoff at the Jews, then ? "
—" No superstitions have I."—" But I have.   I 'm somewhat weaker,
One of the common-place crowd.   Excuse me ; I 'll talk with you later."

MÆCENAS AND RUINS OF HIS VILLA.

—Ah! that this day of darkness e'er should have risen upon me!
Here the rogue vanishing, leaves me powerless under the plowshare.
Now the other's opponent meets him with loud exclamation:
" Where are you going, you scoundrel?—Will you, sir, witness the summons?"
Gladly I give him my ear.   He drags my foe to the court-house,
Noise and confusion abounding.—And so Apollo preserved me.

—Katharine H. Austin.

We were so curious as to follow the poet, and have, in conse-
quence, come back to the Temple of Castor.   But now he has suddenly vanished from sight into the crowded Tuscan Street (*Vicus
Tuscus*).   We will not seek him, for we know that he likes to be alone.

But I will lead you from the forum to the Palatine Hill (*Mons*

Palatinus) near by, to the hill upon which the poor hut of Faus'tulus must have stood, which later bore the stately palace of the Cæsars.

> " The Palatine, proud Rome's imperial seat,
> (An awful pile) stands venerably great :
> Thither the kingdoms and the nations come
> In supplicating crowds to learn their doom ;
> To Delphi less th' inquiring worlds repair,
> Nor does a greater God inhabit there :
> This sure the pompous mansion was design'd
> To please the mighty rulers of mankind ;
> Inferior temples rise on either hand,
> And on the borders of the palace stand,
> While o'er the rest her head she proudly rears,
> And lodged amidst her guardian gods appears."
> —*Claudian* (*Addison's Translation*).

So we go up by the Temple of Castor and Pollux to the modern highroad and to the present entrance-gate of the hill. That arch at the summit of the Sacred Street, which your eyes have frequently sought, is the Arch of Titus, "which, even in its restored condition, is the most beautiful monument of the kind remaining in Rome. Its Christian interest is unrivalled, from its having been erected by the Senate to commemorate the taking of Jerusalem, and from its bas-reliefs of the seven-branched candlestick and other treasures of the Jewish temple. Hawthorne says: "Standing beneath the Arch of Titus, and amid so much ancient dust, it is difficult to forbear the commonplaces of enthusiasm, on which hundreds of tourists have already insisted. Over the half-worn pavement, and beneath this arch, the Roman armies had trodden in their outward march, to fight battles, a world's width away. Returning victorious, with royal captives and inestimable spoil, a Roman triumph, that most gorgeous pageant of earthly pride, has streamed and flaunted in hundred-fold succession over these same flagstones, and through this yet stalwart archway. It is politic, however, to make few allusions to such a past ; nor is it wise to suggest how Cicero's feet may have stepped on yonder stone, or how Horace was wont to stroll

SENATVS
POPVLVS·QVE·ROMANVS
DIVO·TITO·DIVI·VESPASIANI·F
VESPASIANO·AVGVSTO·

PALATINE.

ARCH OF TITUS AND THE AMPHITHEATRE.

TEMPLE OF VENUS.

near by, making his footsteps chime with the measure of the ode
that was ringing in his mind.   The very ghosts of that massive and
stately epoch have so much density that the people of to-day seem
the thinner of the two, and stand more ghost-like by the arches and columns, letting the rich sculpture be discerned through their ill-compacted substance." But, pursuing our way up the Palatine, at the right of our path now rise up, in three stories, high arches, and daily new walls come to light here.

CALIGULA.

These ruins belong to the immense palace which Cal-ĭg'ula built at the northwest side of the Palatine. The front of this palace faced the forum. For Suetō'nius says, in the biography of this emperor, that he had extended this side of the Pala-tine, by the help of mighty buttresses, to the forum, and had made the Temple of Castor and Pollux a vestibule of the royal palace. Often the emperor placed himself between the celestial brothers, and allowed himself to be worshipped by the passers-by.   We go through the principal modern entrance, which formerly led to the gardens of the Farnese family, and soon come, after turning to the right at the end of the high staircase, to the Hill of Victory.

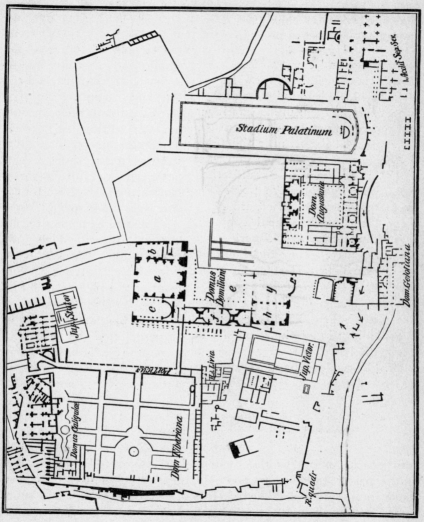

PLAN OF A PART OF THE PALATINE HILL

The top of the Palatine was united with the lowest part of the forum and the surrounding valley, the so-called Vela'brum, by this passage. This Caligula overarched with his extended buildings; and so it happens that we now, at the right and left, look into rooms large and small which have served for the apartments of the royal servants and guards. In some the stone beds are still preserved which are found elsewhere in the Roman guard houses. In others all the furniture is wanting; in only a few have the decorations of ceiling and walls been partially preserved.

If we venture as near the side of the hill as possible, we have just below us the Temple of Castor and Pollux, and over to the west the hill on which stands the Capitoline Temple of Jupiter. From this northwestern point of the Palatine, Caligula bridged over the valley which separated him from his brother (!) Jupiter. Very often he had held conversation with the divinity of the capitol, mysteriously whispering in his ear, and receiving answers in the same way. They did not end without some altercations, for the insane king at last cried out: "Either lift thou me or I will thee," ("῎Η μ᾽ ἀνάειρ᾽ ἢ ἐγὼ σέ." Il., xxiii., 724.) Yet he suffered himself to be quieted again through the invitation of the god to live with him. In order to carry out this command as soon as possible, he united the two hills by means of the famous bridge; (later he laid the foundation for a palace on the Capitoline hill itself.) Three high brick walls still stand at the foot of the Palatine, which apparently belonged to the foundations of that wonderful passage.

Naturally, the bridge must have gone close over the roof of the *Basilica Julia*, and so it might have happened that the capricious ruler, when he visited the capitol, threw gold from the roof of the judgment hall to the people below. On this account, when he had exhausted the public treasury, through his thoughtless extravagance, he condescended on New Year's Day to accept gifts from his subjects, and most graciously received the richest gifts at the entrance of his palace. It is a hard but deserved judgment that all the colossal undertakings of this prince, who seemed always to plan what was foolish, have either entirely vanished or are destroyed past recognition.

A level path went along the northwest side of the hill. Before this side was occupied by royal residences many illustrious Romans had already built their houses there; for the Palatine, with its reminders of the origin of the city, was always a favorite quarter. Three famous orators lived upon the hill— Crassus, Hortensius, and Cicero; also the latter's client, Milo, and his opponent, Clodius. Cicero had bought a place here for about a quarter of a million; but his good neighbor Clodius surpassed him, and paid $600,000 for his. Where each of these possessions lay can no longer be established with certainty; from Cicero's own evidence only this can be

HORTENSIUS.

learned: that his house could be seen from the open place here, and that it was in the neighborhood of the official residence of the chief priest (Pontifex Maximus), which was situated at the forum, between the Temple of Castor and the Palatine.

Along the whole region which runs parallel with the *Velabrum*, ancient and modern walls meet our way, which, however, awaken no great interest. It is only at the southwestern angle of the hill that we encounter a remarkable ruin—the remains of the oldest wall of Rome. The material for the well-hewn blocks of stone was obtained from the Palatine Hill itself. A portion of the wall, some five layers, is still standing upright, in which the stones are placed alternately length and breadth-wise, without mortar. The greatest thickness of the wall is fourteen feet, a thickness which was very effective where the wall made a right angle. In the construction of the first fortification, such a wall was built around the whole hill, inclosing an irregular quadrangle, the so-called *Roma Quadrā′ta*. From this point remains of the ancient wall are seen at other places along the edge of the hill, but at this particular point it is best preserved ; while, for example, beside the main gate, in front of the Temple of Jupiter Stator, it is fast crumbling to pieces.

This part of the Palatine along which we have just passed the Romans called *Ger′malus* (which is said by Varro to be derived from *germani*, twins), in remembrance of the wonderful rescue of the twins, Romulus and Remus. The Tiber near by, into whose raging flood they were to have been thrown, had just at that time overflowed its banks, and filled the hollows between the Capitoline, Palatine, and Av′entine Hills. So the royal servants put the basket with the two brothers into the shallow water at the first convenient slope of the hill, where a fig-tree projected from the water, supposing that the little ones would meet their death here as well as in the main current. At that time this region was still very wild, with wolves roaming in the forest. Is it any wonder, then, if one of these hungry animals, hearing the children cry, trotted thither to spy out the unexpected booty ? But at sight of the weeping brothers the she-wolf forgot her fierceness, herself, and her young ones, and nourished the two hungry creatures with her milk. Faustulus, who had just then stepped out of the thicket, observed this singularly affecting group with astonishment, carried the children home to his Laurentia, and reared them strong, brave lads.

" They were doomed by a bloody king : they were doomed by a lying priest :
They were cast on the raging flood : they were tracked by the raging beast.
Raging beast and raging flood alike have spared the prey ;
And to-day the dead are living, the lost are found to-day.
*   *   *   *   *   *   *   *   *
The troubled river knew them, and smoothed his yellow foam,
And gently rocked the cradle that bore the fate of Rome.
The ravening she-wolf knew them, and licked them o'er and o'er,
And gave them of her own fierce milk, rich with raw flesh and gore."

                                          —*Macaulay.*

THE BRONZE WOLF (Cic., in Cat. III., 19).

Below our feet lies the valley between the Palatine and Aventine
Hills, in which, during the celebration of games, the young Romans
seized and carried off the daughters of the Sā'bines. From the top
of the Palatine down to the circus there was a stairway, called Cacus,
probably in honor of that Cacus who is said to have stolen Hĕr'cu-
lēs's cattle and driven them to his cave in the Aventine. We can no
longer ascend the steps, as most of them have been destroyed, and
besides, we must not yet leave the southern slope ; there are still
many things here to be seen.

On the left appear many traces of private houses, which show that the Romans were fond of living in this neighborhood. For it was no small gratification to a Roman to be able to view the sports in the *circus* from the roof of his house. The imperial palaces, which completely occupied the rest of the hill, never extended to this region. It seems to me quite natural that imperial freedmen, especially, should themselves have purchased property in the vicinity of the Palatine, and this also explains how Augustus could look at the races in the circus from the residences of his friends and freedmen. Caligula regaled himself with the lively scenes in the valley from the Gelo'tian house, (*Dŏ'mus Gelotia'na*). The adjective *gelotiana*, derived from the name of a former inhabitant, was retained even after the rebuilding of the house, to distinguish it from the other parts of the palace.)

The arrangements of the house, of which there are still remains, indicate that it dates from the time of Hadrian, and it is quite in accordance with the character of this emperor that he should have founded a school (*paed'agŏ'gium*) here. In an establishment of this kind, however, you must not imagine a Latin school, nor even a gymnasium, but rather a training school, where youths were instructed in polite manners and in the arts of the courtier. These institutions often turn out the most influential courtiers. For this reason aspiring young men were eager to enter, as we learn from the epitaph of a boy of seventeen, a student in one of these schools. He complains of being torn away from his studies too soon : "*Discessi ab urbe in Praetorio Caesaris, ubi dum studerem, fata mihi inviderunt raptumque ab arte tradiderunt hoc loco.*" The youths whose education was being provided for by the emperor (*pueri Cae'sarum*) are repeatedly mentioned in inscriptions, as are also their teachers (the *praeceptores Caesarum* or *paedagogi puerorum*).

In this *paedagogium* we still recognize the pillared court, flanked on opposite sides by small rooms. Only those on the left, grouped around an ancient salon (*exĕ'dra*), are preserved. They excite a peculiar interest on account of the inscriptions found on the walls.

HADRIAN.

The words scratched on the wall are for the most part the work of young men leaving the *paedagogium*, as, for example, the following:

CORIN
      THVS
           EXIT
               DE PEDAGO
                   GIO.
                        (Corinthus is leaving school.)

The method of instruction in this *paedagogium* does not seem to have suited Corinthus, whose departure is recorded at another place. His twice-occurring "*exit*" sounds very much like a triumph at having at last outgrown the power of the pedagogues.

Many names have appended to them the letters ₊VDN, and several times the word beginning with V is written out in full, *verna* (a slave born in his master's house), so that the abbreviations must be read *verna domini nostri* ("a *verna* of our master"). In this imperial institute the children of the court-servants chiefly were trained, but they did not constitute the only inhabitants of the house; there was in it also a guard of soldiers, rendered necessary on account of the isolated position of the hill. Some of these also have immortalized (!) their names, at the same time disclosing by the addition of "*peregrī'nus*" ("foreigner"), that they belonged to that part of the army which consisted of foreigners. Since these had their rendezvous on the neighboring Cæ'lian hill, it is probable that the post in the *Domus Gelotiana* consisted of soldiers from that place. There must have been in the *paedagogium*, also, servants for the heavy work, and slaves intrusted with the management of the whole establishment.

It is quite a lively scene that is unfolded before our eyes in these deserted chambers. In the small, cool rooms the boys are learning their lesson (*pensum*); yonder, at the entrance, soldiers are loitering about, while others are sitting in airy *exedra*, relating to each other loquaciously (*multis cum verbis*) their various adventures. During the narration of these tales, probably not quite new, the listeners had time to think of other things and scratch their "happy thoughts" on the walls. Sometimes they drew pictures of circus-horses, fighters in nets, or other reminiscences from the arena.

The pupils appear to have been as fond at that time of teasing each other as they are to-day. At any rate, in a small room is the name LIBĀ'NVS, and under it, in a different hand, is written EPISCOPVS. In still another place is repeated: LIBANVS EPI. Libanus, without doubt, had the bad habit of "telling on" his fellow pupils, and so they nicknamed him (*episcopus*)the "overseer." I do not think it can be inferred from this nickname that he was a Christian. Perhaps the one who wrote the Greek word underneath had just learned it, and felt glad that it suited the unpopular Libanus so well.

More uncouth, but more good natured, is the joke on the wall in the last room, where, with a few bold strokes, the picture of an ass turning a mill-stone is scratched into the plaster, and below it are these words : (*Labora, aselle, quomodo ego laboravi, et proderit tibi*) "work, little donkey, as I have, and it will do you good." This witticism may have been perpetrated by a slave who formerly had to turn the mill himself, and is now leisurely looking at the donkey doing it. But I would rather ascribe the jest to one of the departing pupils. He has become " soured," and is now laughing at the complaints of one of those who must remain, and so draws this neat little picture behind his back.

Of all these scrolls the well-known caricature of the crucifixion has become the most noted. To a cross drawn by a few lines is affixed a man with a head of an ass, and, by his side, as if engaged in prayer, is a horribly deformed man, with these words : (Ἀλεξάμενος σέβετε [σέβεται] θεόν) " Alexam'enos worships God." As Alexamenos in another inscription is called a "*fidē'lis*" ("faithful one"), it is established, beyond a doubt, that here a Christian was mocked by his rude companions because he was not afraid to pray in their presence. It was cast in the face of the Jews originally that they worshipped an ass's head. In the wilderness they were said to have followed the wild asses to see where they went to drink, and to have worshipped the ass afterward in the temple in thankfulness for this guidance. And since the Christians were regarded at first as a sect of the Jews, they had to endure this senseless reproach. Tertŭl'lian, in his defence of Christianity, repels this imputation with much force. The "mock crucifix" belongs to the time of this church father, at the end of the second or beginning of the third century, and shows that the habit, wide-spread at that time, of deriding the Christians, had penetrated even into the youthful circle of the *paedagogium*. These rooms also have for us great interest from the belief which many have that they are those once occupied by the Prætorian guard which had St. Paul in custody. "The close of the Epistle to the Ephesians contains a remarkable example of the forcible imagery of St. Paul. Considered simply in itself, the description of the Christian's armor is one of the most striking passages in the sacred volume. But if we view it in connection with the circumstances with which the Apostle was surrounded, we find a new and living emphasis in his enumeration of all the parts of the heavenly panoply,—the belt of sincerity and truth, with which the loins are girded for the spiritual war,—the breastplate of that righteousness, the inseparable links of which are faith and love,—the strong sandals, with which the feet of Christ's soldiers are made ready, not for such errands of death and despair as those on which the Prætorian soldiers were daily sent, but for the universal message of the Gospel of Peace,—the large shield of confident trust, wherewith the whole man is protected, and whereon the fiery arrows of the wicked one fall harmless and dead,—the close-fitting helmet, with which the hope of salvation invests the head of the believer,—and finally the sword of the spirit, the Word of God, which, when wielded by the great Captain of our Salvation, turned the tempter in the wilderness to flight, while in the hands of His chosen Apostle, with whose memory the sword seems inseparably associated, it became the means of establishing Christianity on the earth. All this imagery becomes doubly forcible if we remember that when St. Paul wrote the words he was chained to a soldier, and in the close neighborhood of military sights and sounds. The appearance of the Prætorian guards was familiar to him ; as his ' chains,' on the other hand, so he tells us in the succeeding epistle, became well known throughout the whole Prætorium."—*Conybeare and Howson.*

The *Domus Gelotiana* stands at the end of a hollow which formerly separated the northwestern part of the Palatine from the southeastern. Up to this we have passed along the northwestern edge of the hill, and are now entering on that part which extends toward the southeast, which was not occupied till later times by imperial buildings. Septimius Severus built himself a palace here similar to the one of Caligula at the north side. Endless rows of lofty arches and innumerable chambers engage our attention here, but it is no longer possible to tell the original use of each room. Lofty corridors, small, damp rooms, baths, splendid halls, succeed one another, and we are glad to reach the summit of the ruins without losing our way. Here we stand on the floor of the main hall, and the gloomier our way was through the lower story, the more charming is the view from above. Irresistibly attracted by the landscape which is spread out before us, we forget the ruins beneath our feet. Directly in front of us, toward the Tiber, is the Av'entine, now the most deserted of all the hills, being occupied by monasteries and vineyards only; and, although it has no stately palaces and magnificent churches, the eye rests with satisfaction on its many green gardens. Far toward the south stretches the forsaken *Campa'gna*, traversed by the *Via Ap'pia*, with its ruins and tombs.

One must see it to feel its attractiveness. To me it appears, with its monuments and half-broken down arches of ancient aqueducts, like the lonely potters-field. No matter how warm the sun shines down upon it, how clear and blue the sky above it, it always retains its melancholy hues ; only a sad halo is diffused over it. How gayly the Alban hills rise up in the distance, and how charmingly the villages and towns nestle on their slopes.

"Alba, thou findest me still, and, Alba, thou findest me ever,
Now from the Capitol steps, now over Titus's Arch,
Here from the large grassy spaces that spread from the Lat'eran portal,
Towering o'er aqueduct lines lost in perspective between,
Or from a Vat'ican window, or bridge, or the high Cŏl-ĭsē'um,
Clear by the garlanded line cut of the flavian ring.
Beautiful can I not call thee, and yet thou hast power to o'ermaster,
Power of mere beauty ; in dreams, Alba, thou hauntest me still."
—*A. H. Clough.*

But above and beyond the hills tower up, skirting the horizon, the jagged, treeless summits of the Apennīnes, already clad in their wintry garments of snow.

If we turn our eyes back from this distant view, they will rest in the near vicinity of the most stupendous ruin of Rome, on the Flavian Amphitheatre or Colisē'um. The side toward us has disappeared down to the first story, while on the other the circles tower up one above the other to the highest gallery. From our position we have a view into the interior of the structure. It rises up before us with its gigantic masonry like a city on the slope of a hill.

> " Arches on arches ! as it were that Rome,
>   Collecting the chief trophies of her line,
> Would build up all her triumphs in one dome,
>   Her Coliseum stands ;
> *   *   *   *   *   *   *
> A ruin—yet that ruin !   From its mass
>   Walls, palaces, half-cities, have been reared ;
> Yet oft the enormous skeleton ye pass
>   And marvel where the spoil could have appeared
> Hath it indeed been plundered, or but cleared ?
>   Alas ! developed, opens the decay,
> When the colossal fabric's form is neared :
>   It will not bear the brightness of the day,
> Which streams too much on all years, man, have reft away."
>   —*Byron.*

" This vast building was erected in A. D. 72, upon the site of the reservoir of Nero, by the Emperor Vespasian, who built as far as the third row of arches, the last two rows being finished by Titus after his return from the conquest of Jerusalem. It is said that 12,000 captive Jews were employed in this work, as the Hebrews in building the Pyramids of Egypt, and that the external walls alone cost a sum equal to 17,000,000 francs. It consists of four stories, the first Dŏr'ic, the second Iŏn'ic, the third and fourth Corĭn'thian. Its circumference is 1641 feet, its length 287, its width 182, its height 157." " The dedication of the Coliseum afforded to Titus an opportunity for a display of magnificence hitherto unrivalled. A battle of cranes with dwarfs representing the pigmies was a fanciful novelty, and might afford diversion for

a moment; there were combats of gladiators, among whom women were included, though no noble matron was allowed to mingle in the fray; and the capacity of the vast edifice was tested by the slaughter of five thousand animals in its circuit. The show was crowned with the immission of water into the arena, and with a sea-fight representing the contests of the Cor-inthians and Cor-cyreans, related by Thucȳd'ĭdēs.'' During the games

VESPASIAN.

and shows there was still more to be seen from this height. Then, even early in the morning, the people swayed hither and thither in the long rows of seats in the *Circus Măx'imus*, which lay between the Palatine and Av'entine, in order to secure the best seats; and in the boarding-houses and inns there were lively scenes. "The circus was intended for chariot-races and horse-races, and is said to

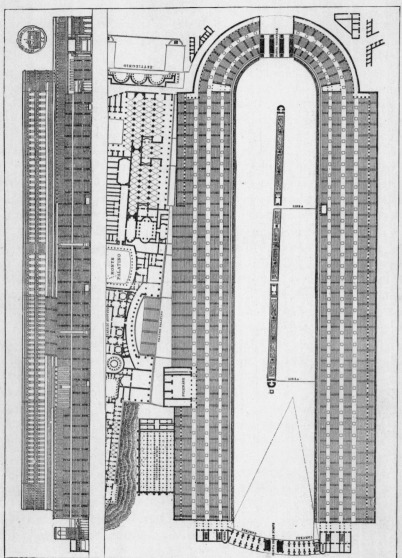

have been first instituted by Tarquinius Priscus, after his conquest
of the Latin town of *Apiolæ*. It was a vast oblong, ending in a
semi-circle, and surrounded by three rows of seats, termed col-
lectively *cā'vea*. In the centre of the area was the low wall called
the *spīna*, at each end of which were the *mētae*, or goals. Between
the metæ were columns supporting the *ŏva*, egg-shaped balls, and
delphī'nae, or dolphins, each seven in number, one of which was
put up for each circuit made in the race. At the extremity of the
circus were the stalls for the horses and chariots called *car'cĕrēs*.
At one time this circus was capable of containing 385,000
persons." It must have had a peculiar charm for a Roman to
watch, in eager suspense, the different parties adorned with their
respective colors, and to be able to follow the green, blue, red, and
white charioteers in their headlong course.

For this reason Septimius Severus built himself, on this side of
the palace, a spacious lodge, from which he could completely survey the games. To this lodge were joined small chambers, of
which a rotunda is particularly noticeable. In the walls are still
seen the niches which were adorned with statues. Into this splendid hall the emperor may have retreated with his friends during
the intervals to recover from the excitement of the games.

The valley, which once was filled with the cries and applause
of a crowd of anxious spectators, has now become silent. The

SEVERUS.

rows of stone benches have disappeared.
The place where once the *car'cĕrēs* confined the restless horses is now occupied
by quite a modern building—a gas factory!
And on the ancient race-course itself, where
once rushed along the Roman two-horse
chariots (*bigae*) rope-makers are now with
careful steps twisting their many-stranded
ropes.

Septimius Severus was very fond of building. We are informed
by his biographer, Sparti'ānus, that, in addition to his new build-

ings, he restored all the public buildings of Rome that had been damaged. His palace he is said to have located on this side of the Palatine, not only for convenience of residence, but also for the purpose of showing his countrymen (he was African) who might approach the city by the Via Appia, how powerful a monarch he was. And this impression he strengthened still more by the so-called *Sĕptizō'nium*, an edifice of seven stories, three of which remained till the time of Sixtus V.

This singular building was finished 203 A. D., after the emperor's return with his victorious army from Asia, where he probably conceived the idea of such a tower. At any rate, the seven stories remind us of the well-known ruins in Babylon, whose terraces were adorned with various colors, and dedicated to seven planets. Now it has all vanished.

I do not, however, purpose to write to you of that which has been destroyed, but rather to teach you to understand that which has survived the storms of time. Unfortunately, we cannot make the circuit of the whole Palatine, as there are still two cloisters on the hill whose gates are closed against us. Let us retrace our steps, therefore, to the *Domus Gelotiana*, and while returning cast a brief glance at the *Stadium*.

By *Stā'dium* is meant a race-course, in which runners, boxers, and wrestlers exhibit their skill. Athletes originally were not admired by the Romans. The first were introduced into Rome in 186 by Fulvius Nobilior. The glădiatorial contests were better suited to the rude tastes of the time. But the more Greek culture found its way into Rome, and the oftener Roman youths went to Greece and visited the gymnasiums (*Palae'stra*), the more athletic sports came into vogue. At first they were held in temporary race-courses or in the circus. Domitian established a stone *Stadium* in the *Campus Martius*, which had a capacity of about thirty thousand. This one on the Palatine appears also to date from the reign of Domitian, and, when we consider his passionate fondness for shows of every kind, it is not surprising that he should have built himself another near his palace on the Palatine. At that time all young men practised the Greek games. Boxing and vaulting were fashionable. It is a little singular, to be sure, that the two court poets, Stā'tius and Martial, who in other respects could not sufficiently celebrate the splendors of their master's reign, make no mention of a *Stadium* on the Palatine. Perhaps they expected us to take the existence of one for granted, since every wealthy Roman had a place for gymnastics near his villa, or perhaps Domitian was unable to finish it.

You can yet see where the straight line was where the athletes began their race, and the curve (σθενδόνη) which closed the upper end of the course. The seats evidently rose in tiers toward the walls, but the plan of the *Stadium* itself was entirely changed by later alterations. The larger part was transformed into an oval space which certainly was still large enough for gymnastic exercises, while the other part was turned into a pillared court. It is probable that the whole Stadium was arranged rather for the private use of the imperial family. The princes took vigorous exercise in all sorts of games, and then refreshed themselves in the shady corridors of the court, or sought repose in the adjacent halls.

Our road now leads us up to the summit of the Palatine, where there was formerly, as has been already stated, a valley. Domitian, no longer satisfied with the old palace, wished to prepare himself a site for a new one, and so filled up the hollow between the hills, thus obtaining a large level surface for his palace, the private houses being torn down and used as foundations for the new building. Several of these old subterranean walls, with traces of their former adornment, may still be seen. A portion of the Palace of Augustus also was destroyed at that time, for here must have been the site of the first imperial residence.

The house of Augustus's parents was on the Palatine, but the exact locality (which was known by the name of "*Ad Capita Bubula*") is unknown to us. Later, Augustus lived near the forum,

AUGUSTUS.

in a house which he had purchased from the Orator Hortensius. Suetonius tells us that it was a very modest dwelling, having only short colonnades, and rooms unadorned either with marble or artistic mosaics. This simplicity exactly suited the new occupant. For more than forty years he remained in Rome, both summer and winter, although the climate during the cooler season did not at all agree with him. For the purpose of having the officers of the government at hand, he purchased several of the neighboring houses, and united them with his own. Besides this, he built a magnificent temple to Apollo on that portion of his property where a thunderbolt had struck. At the same time he established a Greek and Latin library.

On becoming chief priest (*Pon'tifex Măx'imus*), he converted his house into state property, that he might remain here as high priest ; for he was not willing to remove to the residence set apart by the state for the Pontifex, the *Regia*, because he was striving to turn away the attention of the people from the Forum of the Republic to the hill of the emperor. The outline of his house has been traced from the foundation walls, which were discovered during the restoration of the French nunnery. But from the drawings alone it is impossible to indicate the purposes of the several apartments, the ruins themselves being no longer accessible.

Not far from the house of Augustus (*Domus Au'gustā'na*), according to ancient descriptions, was that of Tiberius (*Domus Tiberiā'na*); the site of this is also for the most part covered by modern buildings, the gloomy walls being concealed by charming gardens with blooming rose-hedges. Only that side of the palace toward the *Circus* has been laid bare.

Tiberius also was born on the Palatine, probably in the small house immediately behind the palace. This is the so-called house of Livia. It is especially celebrated on account of its well-preserved wall paintings, and has the arrangements of a Roman private house. Behind the " front room," the *ā'trium*, we enter the *tăb'linum*, which is flanked on both sides by small chambers, the so-called *ā'lae*. The south side is occupied by a richly decorated space that may have served as a dining hall (*triclin'ium*), while the eastern part was used for domestic purposes.

TIBERIUS.

It is noticeable that there is a descent from the entrance hall, the *vestĭb'ulum*, into the *ā'trium*, but it is not probable that this was so originally. The surroundings of the house must have changed through the elevation of the ground by modern buildings.

As Tiberius built his palace beside his father's, he was loth to tear the latter down, but rather preserved the low-lying, modest dwelling as best he could, and gave it to his mother Livia as a "widow's portion." Later, the residence passed into the possession of the family of Germăn'icus.

Tiberius himself lived in the new palace, opposite to the old palace of Augustus. It had an unobstructed view of the Forum and the Capitol. Nothing is known of its interior. On the side toward the house of Livia, a row of arched chambers has been excavated, whose walls were defaced and more or less scribbled over. The import of the words and drawings makes it probable that this was the station-house for the palace guards.

The great fire in the reign of Nero made fearful havoc in this region, the Tenth Ward of the city, to which the Palatine belonged. Part of the walls naturally remained standing, and so the

INTERIOR OF A ROMAN HOUSE.

royal palace (*palatium*) could be restored in a short time. Găl′ba afterward lived in the *palatium*, and with him three of the most influential men of Rome—Titus Vĭn′ius, Cornelius Lā′co, and the freedman Ĭcĕlus—whom the people jestingly called the emperor's tutors.

GALBA.

The Emperor Galba was to have been murdered in his own house, and yet Otho feared the watchfulness of the body-guards; so, on the day on which he intended, with the aid of the dissatisfied prætorians, to execute the *coup d'état,* he had the false report spread that the disorders in the camps were over, and he himself killed. Having thus induced the credulous Galba to go down to the forum without trustworthy protection, he had him surprised and killed.

Otho himself had affectionately greeted the emperor in the morning, and had then, as Tacitus says, under the pretense of having, with several experts, to look at a house offered for sale, hastened away "through the Palace of Tiberius into the Velabrum, thence to the Golden Milestone by the Temple of Saturn"—("*per Domum Tiberianam in Velabrum, inde ad milliarium aureum sub Aedem Saturni.*") Suetonius affirms that he made his way through the rear portion of the *palatium.* From a comparison of these two passages, it is seen that the Palace of Augustus at that time was still used as the principal place of assembly for the Senate, and that the Palace of Tiberius was looked upon rather as the private residence of the emperor.

OTHO.

The first state paper which the new Emperor Otho signed was an appropriation of about twenty-five thousand dollars for the completion of Nero's Palace, which stretched from the Palatine to the Esquiline. But the ninety-five days of his reign did not suffice to finish this golden palace. The reign of Vitellius, also, was too short for that purpose. Vespasian's army entered Rome too soon.

VITELLIUS.

Vitellius, who, in his perplexity, was entirely dependent on the caprice of his soldiers, took no part in the storming of the Capitol, but calmly surveyed the exciting contest and the conflagration from the Palace of Tiberius, in which he was feasting at the time.

The Flavian emperors carried the excessively extended Palace of Nero no further. As a favor to the pleasure-loving people, they erected the colossal amphitheatre, which has been named after them, in a hollow between the Palatine, Cælian, and Esquiline Hills. Vespasian appears not to have had much admiration for the Palatine, and did not live there, but in the gardens of Sallust, near the Pincian and Quiri'nal.

In the reign of Titus another fire broke out, which considerably injured the Capitol. Titus considered it his first duty to repair these new damages, and to give every assistance in his power to the unfortunate cities of Campania. Domitian was the first to build a new palace for his family. He was far from desirous of restoring the Palace of the odious Caligula, and preferring to live in the vicinity of the Palace of Augustus, he built a new palace on the level ground, made by filling up the hollow, as has already been mentioned. Although this palace was not of so gigantic proportions as that of Nero, it was scarcely inferior to it in splendor.

This is the only palace on the Palatine whose interior arrangements are still easily traceable. On the side toward the forum there was a broad stairway, but all traces of this are lost in the terraced ground. The vestibule is not a narrow passage, like that in the house of Livia, but a broad landing-place, where the stairway began. Here the degenerate Romans waited until their " Jupiter " saw fit to give them an audience. As the troops of clients in ancient times assembled at the atrium of their "patron" to greet him and accompany him to his business in the forum, so now the nobles wait at the door of the Palatium for permission from the dread tyrant to enter. All the events of the day have been discussed ; the rich material for conversation afforded by the new plays introduced by the emperor, has long since been exhausted ; every outbreak of ill-humor on the part of the master has been traced to its source ; when, finally, the large doors of the reception hall are thrown open, and a troop of servants, dressed in white, step forth upon the threshold to survey, with grim faces, the waiting crowd. For, not every one is admitted to the presence of the emperor. It costs the less-esteemed

TITUS.

knight much trouble and many a *denarius* before he can surmount every obstacle.

To-day he has been fortunate enough, for the first time, to enter these halls. He is dazzled by the splendor. It surpasses all his expectations. He has scarcely the courage to step over the threshold, which consists of an immense block of Grecian marble ; but one glance into the interior tells him that he cannot begin to examine everything in detail ; there is too much of beauty to be seen. He is most pleased with the pillars of Phrygian and Numidian marble, with which the walls are adorned. The bases, and especially the capitals, are so elaborately carved and so rich in their forms that they appear to him much more beautiful than the simple ones of the ancient temples. Behind the portico the walls are relieved by niches, from which gods and heroes look down on the actions of feeble mortals.

But our knight, at present, does not desire to admire Hercules and Bacchus and the rest of the statues; he wants, above all, to see him whom the poets have compared to the father of the gods. Yonder, on his lofty seat, he sits enthroned, opposite the entrance, proud and gloomy, looking down upon those approaching to greet him.

Long time had our ambitious knight to possess his soul in patience before the doors of this hall of the gods were thrown open to him; and now, instead of Jupiter, he verily thinks he sees before him the gods of the lower world. Timidly he drops his eyes in the presence of the angry and suspicious glance of Domitian. From the chamber on the left comes forth the fragrance of incense which had been burned yonder on the small altar to the genius of the emperor. Did the tyrant in the enjoyment of all these honors have some conception of his human weakness? Was it on that account that his forehead was clouded, his lips compressed? The knight knew not, but he felt that here every movement, every look, might furnish an occasion for speedy death. The floor with the costly marble begins to burn under his feet, and he notices with terror that only a few individuals approach the throne to greet the tyrant with a morning kiss.

Yet there are only a few who are deemed worthy of this honor. The people call them the "first friends" of the emperor, and envy them greatly. So our young Roman previously has known no higher aim in life than to be counted among this first class of the "friends" (" amici"), but to-day he can do very well without that happiness; the imperial kiss had no longer any charm for him. He hastens down the stairs of the palace as if awakened from a nightmare, and wishes in his inmost soul that he had never felt the ambition to bid the emperor good morning.

A ROMAN GARDEN SCENE (WALL PAINTING IN POMPEII).

Meanwhile his companions rush upon him with most eager and curious questions: "In what kind of a mood was he?" "What did the *haruspices* announce?" "Whom did he salute with a kiss?" "What expression did his face assume when your name was announced?" Although at that moment it had become so dark to the eyes of the knight that he did not notice anything around him, he nevertheless answered very explicitly all these and other questions of his eager friends, and felt his own importance immensely. When they reached the forum he had forgotten the anguish he had undergone, and even believed that he should soon become one of the most favored of friends.

After the tedious morning solemnities the emperor went to the court-room (c), which was on the right of the *aula regia*. Along both sides of the interior were columns, whilst the space opposite the door was used as a *rostrum*. With its mosaic floor it is as well preserved as if the emperor, supported by his wily counsellors, had decided here only yesterday the most important cases. There is also seen quite a good part of the pretty marble barriers which barely separated the seats of the jurors from the place occupied by the people. "The appeals from the provinces in civil causes were heard, not by the emperor himself, but by his delegates, who were persons of rank; Augustus had appointed one such delegate to hear appeals from each province respectively. But criminal appeals appear generally to have been heard by the emperor in person, assisted by his council of assessors. Tiberius and Claudius had usually sat for this purpose in the forum; but Nero, after the example of Augustus, heard these causes in the imperial palace."

In the private homes of the Romans, the so-called *fauces* united the front part of the house with the *peristylium* and the garden. But as such narrow passages were not used in palaces, Domitian had constructed upon both sides broad halls that grew to the size of rooms (d). Here the servants were permitted to stay. They might also have been used for the keeping of many utensils which were indispensable for the cleaning of the halls. From the passage one

NERO.

entered the court-yard (e), which took in a space of 3,000 square
metres. The floor was cleared, and we can conclude from the relics
found there that costly marble columns had formed, in the interior,
a sort of passage, which gave a cooling shade to the lord and his
aristocratic guests.

Just as the *aula regia* and the adjacent rooms were devoted to
serious business, so were the spaces into which we just entered
reserved for the guests invited to the imperial table. The guests,
adorned in festive togas, were carried in their sedan-chairs to the

side entrance of the palace and hastened, full of expectation, up the few steps which led them immediately to the octagonal reception room (f). There they greeted their friends and looked critically at the new-comers, who gazed with embarrassed looks at the mosaic floor and the ornaments on the walls. Old acquaintances were soon in eager conversation and withdrew mysteriously into the smaller apartments which joined the ante-room upon both sides.

At last the servants called the guests to the repast, and from all sides these thronged to the dining-room, from the lofty doors of which the curtains had been drawn back. Their eyes, which had already become weary in admiring all the treasures, were now in danger of being fairly dazzled on account of the splendor which met their gaze from the gilded ceiling, the lofty granite columns, the artistically patterned mosaic floor. They almost believed they had entered the home of a Mī'das, and only feared that golden refreshments were awaiting them. But when the festive throng of visitors had, at the nod of the emperor, sat down at a thousand tables, then entered in long procession the servants, carrying food and wines, of such exquisite kind that it seemed as if Ce'rēs and Bacchus themselves had come as waiters to the guests.

The host himself, in genial humor, arrayed in purple garments, smiled graciously down upon his company. At least it so appeared to the poet Statius, who had been invited to the imperial table, and related to us afterward what happened there. He cannot praise enough the serene peace and majesty which overspread the countenance of the ruler, and feels like one enchanted at being permitted to feast at table in presence of the all-powerful one; indeed, he imagines himself resting with Jupiter among the stars. Were the other guests equally delighted? Did they also gaze transfigured upon the emperor?

Statius tells us nothing of this, for he speaks only of the most important personages present; that is, of Domitian and himself. Encouraged by the affability of the emperor, he must have approached after the repast the imperial couch to utter his thanks for

MOSAIC.

the invitation, in good wishes that a life without end and a power without limit might be bestowed upon the gracious lord by the gods. Then, proud of his artistic phrases, he hastens home and pours out his enthusiasm in a poem which he means, at a later time, to present to the emperor.

Not all the guests were in such haste. Many were still feasting at the table, though Domitian had already retired; they would have so much liked to learn the secrets of the Court in a confidential conversation with the servants who could be bribed. Others withdrew to the apartment which joins the dining-hall on the right (h). Here bubbled a merry fountain, which poured its waters into an oval marble basin. Four little niches are still seen in this basin, from which, no doubt, some little cupids roguishly smiled down into the mirror-like waters. Round about the fountain were flowers of glowing colors in bloom, and out from the green foliage and rosy leaves looked forth Eros to overlook triumphantly his little kingdom. Now no longer does the gardener tend this bed, but luxuriant plants come up spontaneously and adorn with their fresh foliage this spot which seems like a little boat afloat in the basin. In no room of the lofty palace can one feel so comfortable as in this abode of the nymphs.

A FOUNTAIN (CUPID AND THE GOOSE).

Yet we might, perhaps, have felt different if, in company with the aristocratic Romans, we had entered this alabaster hall from the banquet of the imperial table. Some of them stagger in, intoxicated with wine and pleasure, whilst others sit down quietly by the waters to cool their hot cheeks. One sees in their restless eyes that something torments them, that they fear to have offended the emperor by a thoughtless word or an unguarded look. For Domitian was not always in good humor at table, nor could all enjoy his glances as harmlessly as did Statius. Those occupying an important position in the state were, indeed, obliged to be on their guard.

The emperor paid attention to all present, and often used the time of the repast to watch his invited guests. Then he had dined himself before their arrival, and lay at table on the *triclinium* only to see how his *quirites* would act under the influence of his wines. If the banquet were too long or the company too careful in behavior (!), then he had the different courses served in such haste that the food was rather thrown than placed before the guests.

Still worse did he once treat his tormented courtiers. The hall, formerly so full of splendor, had been draped in black. Near every plate was placed a candle, such as is used in the last services for the dead, and upon a black tablet was written the name of the guest. The servants were clothed in black and served the guests, frightened to death, with food in black utensils. You can imagine in what a state of mind the Senators and first men in the state returned to their homes, and how astonished they were at soon after receiving costly gifts from the emperor, which were to make amends to them for the distress which they had suffered.

Such jests Domitian permitted himself at the time when there were no traces left of the mild disposition and the abstemiousness he had here and there shown in the first year of his reign, whilst now he was bent only upon satisfying his wild passions, and showing his boundless disdain for the upper classes among his people. The punishment was not long in coming. Soon he no longer felt any security; wherever he might be, he imagined himself pursued by an assassin; he started at the slightest noise behind him.

It no longer sufficed that armed guards lay in wait upon the palace stairs, that his chamberlains assured him that he might be without anxiety. He wanted always to be able to overlook the whole open court (*peristylium*), in which he used to take his walk, and therefore he had the walls of the portico (*porticus*) covered with slabs of marble which shone so brightly that whatever happened behind him was reflected by it as by a mirror. Thus were these apartments and halls, in which formerly finely dressed guests feasted at the most luxurious table in Rome, changed into a lonely prison, or (to use the words of the younger Pliny) "a fierce lair, whither he was being driven by terror and haughtiness and the hate of men"—(*saevi secessus, in quos timore et superbia et odio hominum agebatur*).

Between the rear of the Flavian Palace and the southern limit of the mountain lies still a pretty large space, which is bounded on the east by small porticos and two large halls. These open spaces did not, to be sure, belong immediately to the imperial palace of Domitian, but must have had some connection with it. When they were discovered, they were called "Library" and "Academy," and they still bear these names, although one could not prove the justice of these appellations. Both apartments have an entrance from the west. The rear walls were occupied by semi-circular alcoves. In one of them

DOMITIAN.

we can still see the row of seats erected around the walls. We can easily imagine that here the court poets and those who aspired to be so, presented their poems before a chosen public. Graciously accepted poems were then perhaps placed in the Library Building, near by, to find rest there forever more.

The savants could walk into the porticos, and sometimes, in the fresh air, carry on their learned discussions, if by chance it had become too sultry for them in the interior. Perhaps the colonnade, lined by columns, led to the ornamental garden grounds of the emperor, the so-called "*Adonea*," which must have been laid out here toward the east. Some have even supposed that these spaces belonged to a large building for warm baths, which extended as

VIEW ON THE PALATINE.

far as the Stadium. Yet we cannot give proof of this statement until the space between the Flavian Palace and the Stadium has been carefully explored.

The lecture-room has a very fine position at the edge of the hill top, and from its windows one enjoys a wonderful view, which perhaps occupied the thoughts of the listening Romans more than the tedious verses of the endless heroic poems recited there. Upon the plain below the hall one was always sure to find acquaintances, for everybody was glad to go to the *palatium* to hear something new. And very often the conversation there was so entertaining that it was easy to forget for what purpose one had come, and hastening, with quick steps, into the auditorium, he heard only the last of the exquisite (!) verses which the poet was reciting in a hoarse voice to the audience.

After having had this enjoyment one might visit one of the Palatine temples. The next on this side is that of Jupiter Victor, which Fabius vowed during the battle at Sentinum when the victory was almost in the hands of the Samnites. The substructure of the great temple is still in existence, and also the long stairs that led up to it have been replaced, but of the *cella* itself and the columns nothing more is seen.

At a much earlier date had been built a sanctuary to the highest divinity of the state, in front of the oldest Palatine street. This temple also was vowed to the gods in the distress of battle. When the Samnites, with their brave leader, Mettius Curtius, at their head, had driven the Romans over the forum and had pursued them up the hill road as far as the old gate of the *Palatium*, then Romulus raised his sword toward heaven and reminded Jupiter that those were his birds by whose counsel he had founded a city here; would that he might now be pleased to keep the enemy away, at least from this hill, and to remove all fear from the Romans and thus interrupt the disgraceful flight, " Here I vow to thee, Jupiter Stator, a temple, to be a memorial for future generations how through thy timely interference the city was rescued."

In the certainty that his prayer had been heard and accepted he turned towards his soldiers and called : " Here, Romans, Jupiter, greatest and best, commands us to stand and renew the battle," (" *Hinc Romani, Jupiter Optimus Maximus resistere atque iterare pugnam iubet,*") and the ranks ceased to flee. Romulus rushed to the front, the combat began anew and ended in the victory of the Romans, trusting in their God. Jupiter Stator received this promised temple.

M. Attilius Regulus extended this building, in fulfilment of a vow made before Luce'ria in the great battle against the Samnites, 295 B. C. Still at the present day do these ruins left of the restorations of the temples in later republican times remind us how much the Romans cared for these sanctuaries, and how much even the most frivolous emperors embellished them. Before this temple the equestrian statue of Clœlia was erected, so that every one entering the gate near by would be reminded of the Romans' strength and of the bravery of the Roman maiden.

Of the high gate nothing more is seen unless perhaps a ruin of these imperial times marks the place of the ancient gate in front of this temple. It was the *Porta Mugonia*, which was so called because it re-echoed the lowing of the cattle, which the oldest inhabitants of the mountains drove through these gates to pasture.

From here we need to take only a few steps to return to the place where we began our journey. But I should like to take you at least a little distance under the surface of the mountain. An easy stairway leads us from the interior of the Flavian Palace to a subterranean passage, which is paved with rude mosaics; the tint of the walls is yet preserved. This corridor was very practically contrived between the State Palace of Domitian and the house of Tiberius, that through it the emperors might pass to their public offices and work without encountering the curious multitude, standing at any time of the day upon the open square between the palaces. This short passage intersects another passage, which runs nearly the whole length of the east side of the pleasure grounds of Tiberius and Caligula.

Indeed, if we follow the subterranean passage farther toward the south, we can penetrate into the very interior of the mountain. We come then to large caves, whence the material for the most ancient buildings was hewn. But we will not stay long, for it is fearfully dark and very damp in these excavations, aside from the fact that the gray, crumbling wall can hardly be of any interest to you. We hasten back, therefore, to the lighter parts of the passage, and shall see that such a covered passage, lighted only at intervals from the ceiling, must have been a very agreeable place in the hot summer days.

On the day of Caligula's death, a band of Oriental boys, enticed hither by the cool air of the place, must have practiced here their war-dances, in which they wished to excel in the Palatian games.

For this festival, as was customary, a theatre was erected near the northern foot of the Palatine and near the head of the *Via Sacra*, although during the preceding night the emperor had a bad dream —he saw himself standing near the throne of Jupiter, but was kicked to the ground by the god—yet he went nevertheless to the games, and even at one o'clock at noon, he felt no desire to rise for breakfast.

Only by the persuasion of his friends was he induced to leave the house, but did not follow his uncle Claudius or the guards through the entrance of the palace, but entered the *crypta* near the temple of Jupiter to see how those boys were doing their exercises.

CLAUDIUS.

The conspirators used this favorable opportunity to surprise the hated tyrant. Charea, the most influential among them, asked the emperor to give the password. But as the latter gave him an insulting answer, he rushed upon him and thrust his sword deep into his shoulder. Groaning with pain, Caligula tried to escape, but another of the confederates named Cornē′lius Sabī′nus stepped up to him and felled him to the ground. Then the rest fell upon him, encouraging each other to the deed, and in a short time they had killed and mutilated their master.

At sight of the body, bleeding from thirty wounds, they were suddenly seized with terror and anguish, for they feared the revenge of the German body-guard devoted to the emperor. So they hastened down the passage as far as the house of Livia, and remained concealed here until the first excitement in the palace had passed over. We will not follow them into the house, already familiar to us, but will return now through the *porticus* to the entrance, to rest from all we have seen and heard.

Take these pages which I send you from the walls of Rome as a greeting which may spur you on also to follow out, in the future, these traces of antiquity. And, first of all, I should be glad, through my description, to interest you so that in reading the authors you will think more of *where* that happened of which you are reading. The authors, who have lived and written under an Italian sky, are reticent and shy in the foreign school-room. But if we transfer ourselves with them to their home, accompanying them to the market and enter their families, then they grow confiding and social. And, as Hawthorne says: " To a spectator on the spot, it is remarkable that the events of Roman history, and of Roman life itself, appear not so distant as the Gothic ages which succeeded them. We stand in the forum, or on the height of the Capitol, and seem to see the Roman epoch close at hand. We forget that a chasm extends between it and ourselves, in which lie all those dark, rude, unlettered centuries, around the birthtime of Christianity, as well as the age of chivalry and romance, the feudal system, and the infancy of a better civilization than that of Rome. Or, if we remember these mediæval times, they look further off than the

ROME FROM THE JANICULUM (TIME OF AURELIAN).

Augustan age. The reason may be that the old Roman literature survives, and creates for us an intimacy with the classic ages, which we have no means of forming with the subsequent ones."

Learn, therefore, to understand the language of the Romans thoroughly, so as to be able to converse with them at ease, and be assured that you will forget the painful task of the grammar in the joyful intercourse, that you will feel a rare joy if you at a later time shall be permitted to greet on the very spot, as old and dear acquaintances, these temples and houses, these squares and streets, these valleys and hills.

> " Alas, for Tully's voice, and Virgil's lay,
> And Livy's pictured page !—but these shall be
> Her resurrection."

FINIS.